Practically every occasion can benefit from a little humor. Should you need a funny story to liven up the office party, or to open up a sales meeting, or for a wedding anniversary speech, you are likely to find a winner in this book.

# Jokes and Anecdotes
# for All Occasions

## RALPH MARQUARD

**Galahad Books · New York City**

# CONTENTS

# AIRPLANES

THE AIRPLANE WAS GOING through some especially turbulent weather, but the pilot knew he had everything under control. He tried to calm the passengers with soothing words spoken over the loudspeaker system. He also asked the stewardesses to reassure the people that everything would be all right.

One little old lady, however, would not be comforted. The stewardess told her how capable the pilot was and how reliable the plane's technology was, but the woman was still sure she'd never see the ground again.

At a loss, the stewardess finally called on the highest court of appeal. "Just trust in Providence," she said soothingly.

The little old lady's eyes opened even wider. "Is it as bad as that?" she asked.

So many American Jews have been traveling to Israel recently, it is said that El Al, the Israeli airline, has instructed its crew members to learn Yiddish. One stewardess tells of the pilot who really caught the Yiddish idiom in all its flavor.

His message just after a New York takeoff ran:

"*Shalom*, ladies and gentlemen, and welcome to El Al airlines. This is your pilot, Avi Goldberg, wishing you a happy, restful trip, which we certainly expect you to have, God willing. And if by some remote chance we do run into trouble—God forbid!—do not panic, keep calm. Your life belt is under your seat, and if you must put it on, wear it in good health!"

Strong winds buffeted the airplane as it flew through a stretch of turbulent weather, so the "Fasten Seat Belts" sign flashed on. All passengers complied readily, except for one huge Texan who stubbornly refused.

The neophyte stewardess stood by his seat and pleaded with him to follow instructions.

"Young lady," he roared, "for thirty years I've rode everything I ever mounted, and I ain't about to be saddle tied now. Let 'er buck! I'll ride 'er."

# AUTOMOBILES

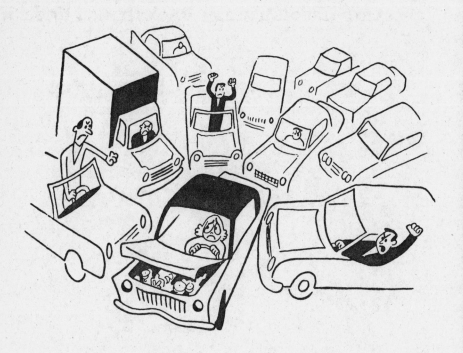

THE OVERRIDING FEAR of every new driver is to find himself stalled in the middle of traffic.

One woman encountered just such a situation, and started her car eleven times in a row only to have the engine fail before she could maneuver out of the intersection. The man behind her blared his horn, even though he saw her predicament.

At the eleventh stall, with the horn loud in her ears, the woman went over to the driver behind her.

"I'm awfully sorry, but I don't seem to be able to start my car," she said pointedly. "If you'll go up there and start it for me, I'll stay here and lean on your horn."

A WOMAN WAS TRYING to maneuver her car out of a parking space. She first crashed into the car ahead, then banged into the car behind, and finally struck a passing delivery truck as she pulled into the street. A policeman who had watched her bumbling efforts approached her. "All right, lady," he demanded, "let's see your license."

"Don't be silly, officer," she replied. "Who'd give *me* a license?"

AN INSURANCE AGENT was teaching his wife how to drive when the brakes of their car failed on a steep downhill grade.

"I can't stop!" shrieked the wife. "What'll I do now?"

"Brace yourself," her husband advised, "and try to hit something cheap."

A DRIVER was out one day testing his late-model Ford, with which he'd been having a lot of trouble. Suddenly, the car stalled and would not move at all.

At that moment, the great Henry Ford himself happened to ride by, and he pulled over to see if he could help.

Ford opened the hood of the car, looked in, and whispered something softly into the engine.

Instantly, the engine sprang into action, humming smoothly.

The car owner was amazed. "Oh, Mr. Ford," he cried, "please tell me what you told the engine so I won't have this trouble again."

Ford smiled and patted his creation fondly. "I just whispered, "Lizzie, this is Henry. Turn over.'"

A WOMAN DRIVING in Brooklyn stopped her car for a red light. However, when the light turned green again, she just stayed right where she was. When the light had changed several times and she still hadn't moved, the traffic policeman finally went over to her and inquired politely, "What's the matter, lady, ain't we got no colors you like?"

A TAXI WAS CREEPING slowly through rush-hour traffic, and the passenger was already late. "Please," he told the driver, "can't you go any faster?"

"Sure I can," the hack replied. "But I'm not allowed to leave the cab."

A TAXI PASSENGER was being buffeted to the right and to the left as his driver careened down the avenue at breakneck speed. When the gentleman was granted an instant to catch his breath, he finally complained to the driver.

"You ain't got no cause to worry," said the man. "I ain't goin' to land back in no hospital now, after eighteen months in one overseas."

Only partially reassured, the rider grumbled, "How dreadful. You must have been seriously wounded."

"Nope. Never got a scratch," grinned the cabbie. "I was a mental case."

BILL WAS FED UP with his gas-eating station wagon, and sold it to his friend Danny for $500. But the next day, Bill began to miss the old crate, and offered to buy it back from Danny for $550. So Danny sold him the car. The following day, he looked up Bill.

"I'm sorry I sold the car back to you, Bill," he said. "I'll give you $600 for it right now."

So, Danny bought the car back. The next day Bill again regretted the sale, and bought it back for $650.

The next day, Danny came to buy the car back, but learned Bill had sold it to his cousin.

"You idiot! Why did you sell it to an outsider?" chided Danny, "especially when we were both making such a great living out of it!"


A TRUCK DRIVER was tooling down a country road in Pennsylvania one afternoon. As there were no other cars in sight, the driver speeded up to a rather carefree rate. A slow-moving car began crossing the intersection up ahead, but he saw it too late and plowed into its rear end.

Unhurt, but seething with fury, a God-fearing Quaker woman climbed out of what had been a brand-new Ford. Almost ready to spit with rage, the woman held onto her religious discipline and slowly walked up to the truck driver.

Then, glaring at him, she said, "When thee gets home to thy kennel tonight, I hope thy mother bites thee."

"I'VE GOT TO get rid of Charlie the chauffeur," complained the husband. "He's nearly killed me four times!"

"Oh!" pleaded his wife, "Give him another chance."

# BEACH

A young man left his wife on the beach for a few minutes while he went to buy some ice cream cones. When he came back, he saw a big crowd gathered around. "What happened?" he asked a bystander.

"Some woman nearly drowned," was the answer. "They're working on her down there."

The young man pushed through the crowd. Sure enough, it was his wife. "What are you doing to her?" he shouted to the lifeguard.

"Giving her artificial respiration," replied the guard.

"Artificial!" howled the young man. "Give her the *real* thing! I'll pay for it."

ON A SWANKY BEACH in Rhode Island, the local constable came up to a cute young thing and said, "Look, you're perfectly within the law wearing that abbreviated bikini, but just tell me, aren't you ashamed of yourself wearing so little clothing?"

The girl replied, "No sir, not at all! If I were," she said glancing down at her shapely thighs, "I'd wear more."

# BIRTHDAYS & ANNIVERSARIES

To CELEBRATE LITTLE HOWIE'S bar mitzvah, Mr. and Mrs. Shapiro sought something unique. The usual catered affairs were a thing of the past. All year long, Howie's friends have been having miniature-golf bar mitzvahs, amusement-park bar mitzvahs, and Broadway-show bar mitzvahs. For weeks, the Shapiros racked their brains trying to come up with something that hadn't been done before.

Finally Mr. Shapiro decided. "We'll have a safari bar mitzvah! Hang the expense! We'll charter a plane for all our friends and relatives and fly to the depths of the jungle."

All the arrangements were made. Soon the great day came. Led by a native African guide, the bar mitzvah party made its way along the safari trail.

They had only been hiking a few minutes when the guide came to an abrupt halt. Impatiently, Mr. Shapiro asked, "What's happened? Why are we stopping?"

The guide replied, "We'll have to wait here for awhile. There's another bar mitzvah right ahead of us."

A MAN AND HIS WIFE were celebrating their 50th wedding anniversary. They invited their two sons to the celebration, but neither of them showed up. They didn't even bother to send a gift or a congratulatory message.

About a month later, the sons paid the old couple a visit and were treated to a sumptuous dinner. They offered the weakest excuses for their failure to attend the Golden Wedding celebration. One of the sons claimed that he was out of town on a business trip, and the other said that he was involved in a golf tournament.

The father and mother were more depressed than impressed. Suddenly, the old man announced, "Boys, I have something to tell you that I've never told you before. The fact is, that although we celebrated our 50th wedding anniversary, your mother and I were never really married."

"What?" shrieked one of his sons, "What you're telling us is that we're bastards!"

"That's right!" asserted the father, "And cheap ones, too!"



AFTER MANY YEARS of not having seen each other, Deborah ran into Rhea at—of all places—a bar mitzvah reception her boyfriend had invited her to.

The women shed tears, and immediately

fell into deep conversation. Suddenly, the bar mitzvah boy walked in, to the applause of the assembled guests.

"Look at that poor boy!" Deborah whispered. "His face is so full of pimples, you could almost throw up looking at him!"

Rhea was scandalized. "It so happens," she announced haughtily, "that that's my boy, David!"

Deborah's face turned bright red, then she asserted effusively, "You know, darling, on him they're becoming."

FOR HIS BIRTHDAY, Mrs. Finkelstein gave her grown-up son Charlie two Dior ties. One was red and the other blue.

On his next visit to his mother, Charlie put on the red tie and strode into the apartment.

His mother took one look at him and sighed, "Ah! The blue one you didn't like."

# BORROWING & LENDING

MRS. GOLD FELL ASLEEP quickly one night, but her husband lay awake tossing and turning. Finally the commotion awoke Mrs. Gold, and she began complaining.

"Harry, what is it? Why are you tossing and turning so, that I can't even get a good night's sleep?"

"Oh, sweetheart," sighed Mr. Gold, "I'm so worried, that's what it is. I borrowed $3000 dollars from Jake Stein across the street, and I thought business was going to get better, but it's worse. The note is due tomorrow, and I've no idea where I'm going to get the money to pay it with."

"Is that what's keeping you awake?" asked Mrs. Gold. And with that, she opened up the window and started screaming, "Jake! Jake!"

In half-a-minute, Jacob Stein was at his window. "What's the matter?" he yelled back.

"Jake," yelled Mrs. Gold, "Abie owes you three grand. The note is due tomorrow. He's been up all night worrying where to get the money, but he can't raise it. Now *you* worry!"

Levy manufactured swimwear. Business was terrible. But Levy thought he saw a last chance to avoid bankruptcy by buying a huge lot of underwear at a very low price. If he could sell it all at a good profit, he'd be all right. So Levy borrowed several thousand dollars from his bank.

Unfortunately, the sales turned out to be slow. What was worse, his bank called him in to ask for the money. He had signed a demand note.

"Mr. Levy," said the bank president, "we'll have to call in your loan. We've no alternative."

"Well," said Levy, "are you yourself perhaps interested in underwear?"

The president laughed. "Mr. Levy, I am not in the least interested in the underwear business."

"Too bad," said Levy, "because as of this week, you're in it."


Abe said to his friend Willie, "Willie, lend me twenty dollars."

Willie took out his wallet and handed Abe a ten dollar bill.

"Willie," said Abe, "I asked you for twenty."

"Yes, I know," said Willie. "This way you lose ten and I lose ten."

A LITTLE BOY asked his father to explain the difference between capital and labor.

"Well, son," the father replied, "If you lend money, that's capital. If you try to get it back, that's labor."



A BUTCHER once went over his accounts and found that one of his customers, the famous Daniel Webster, owed him a substantial sum of money. Calling on the Webster household several times, he received no satisfaction. So he instituted a suit in court to get his payment.

While the suit was pending, Webster happened to meet the butcher on the street one day. The statesman boldly asked, "Why have you not sent around for my order?"

"Why, Mr. Webster," remarked the surprised butcher, "I did not think you wanted to deal with me when I brought this suit."

Webster was not abashed. "Tut, tut," he said. "Sue all you wish, but for heaven's sake, don't try to starve me to death."



Some people will go to great lengths to get out of something they'd rather not do. Others take a more straightforward approach.

An Iowa corn farmer once saw his neighbor coming up the road to visit. The neighbor wanted to borrow the farmer's brand-new ax. The farmer hestitated. Then he said, "Sorry, Jim, I've got to shave tonight."

The farmer's teenage son was mortified. He was close enough to hear the conversation, but he said nothing. Then at the dinner table he asked his father, "Dad, why did you give Jim such a silly excuse when he wanted to borrow the ax?"

His father replied, "If you don't want to do a thing, one excuse is as good as another."

ONE MEMBER of the wealthy Rothschild family was invited to a friend's house for a business meeting. The friend was embarrassed, but explained that he was in need of borrowing some money.

Mr. Rothschild was agreeable, but he did require an endorser, someone who would be prepared to accept responsibility for the loan should the friend default. The man could think of no one. Finally, he was forced to tell his wealthy friend that the only one who might believe in him was God Almighty Himself.

The financier seemed to accept that, and he lent his friend the money, signing on the note, "Endorsed by God Almighty."

Some months went by and Rothschild's friend was back on his feet again, and he went gladly to pay back his debt. But at Rothschild's home, he found that the rich man would not take his money.

"But why not?" he asked.

Rothschild patted his friend on the shoulder. "My dear friend," he said, "the Endorser has already repaid the loan."

In the days of pioneering the wild old West, Jake and Izzy were traveling through Colorado by stagecoach. Suddenly the coach stopped, and Jake realized that robbers were about to stage a hold-up.

Quickly, Jake took some money from his wallet and handed it to his companion. "Izzy," he explained, "here is the fifty dollars I owe you."

"Well congratulations," the real estate agent told the old sharecropper, who had just paid the last installment on a small farm. "I'll make you a deed to the farm now that it's all paid for."

"If it's all the same to you," the sharecropper replied, "I wish you'd give me a mortgage to the place instead."

The astonished real estate agent suggested that the old man didn't know the difference between a deed and a mortgage.

"Well, maybe not," the sharecropper shrugged. "But I owned a farm once and I had a deed and the bank had the mortgage, and the bank got the farm!"

FINKEL HAD FAILED at several business pursuits when he decided to try his hand at opening a grocery store. But he needed capital.

He went to see Mandelbaum in his candy store. Finkel confided his scheme for the grocery to his old friend. He carefully explained that, rather than asking his friends for money, he had gone to the bank. The banker reassured him that there was no problem lending him the money; all he had to do was have some responsible person in the neighborhood sign a note for him. Then the money would be his.

Mandelbaum knew Finkel, and he knew his schemes. So he said, "Finkel, you shouldn't have to borrow money from a bank. What are friends for? How long have we known each other that you should go borrowing money from a bank. I tell you what. I'll give you the money myself. All you have to do is to get that man at the bank to sign on the back of my note, and the money will be yours!"

A butcher was going over his account books and found that Mrs. Levy owed him a sizable sum of money. He called her on the phone several times, but could never get in touch, so he decided to send her a letter.

"Dear Mrs. Levy," he wrote, "please pay up the money that you owe me."

The next week, he received a reply in the mail: "I can't pay right now, but please send me two good chickens, four pounds of hamburger, and six steaks."

The butcher was angry. He wrote again: "Dear Mrs. Levy: I will send your order when you pay up your account."

The reply came the next day: "I can't wait that long!"

A CERTAIN Chicago journalist was infamous for his lethargic manner of debt repayment. One time, a friend at a noted Washington, D.C.

banking house lent the newspaperman a sizable sum, only to find repayment put off indefinitely for one reason or another.

After several months, the Washingtonian decided to travel to Chicago to collect his money. But the same excuses greeted him in person as had greeted him through the mail.

Although the columnist couldn't afford to repay the loan, he decided at least to provide some publicity for his friend, so he ran a notice in his column for the next day:

"Mr. So-and-So, the well-known Washington banker, is in Chicago for a few days looking after some of his permanent investments."

J. F. Williams owed the finance company one thousand dollars. After months of delinquency, he wrote to the company as follows:

"Dear Sir:

"I am sorry that I haven't paid my bill in all these months, and I feel thoroughly ashamed of myself. But I can now pay my bill and hold my head up high. Enclosed find my check to you for the thousand dollars I owe you.

"Yours truly,
"J. F. Williams.

"P.S. This is the kind of a letter I would have written you if I had the money."

The grocer's son had come home from his first year at the university and was anxious to discuss serious subjects with his father. The grocer was pleased.

"Father," the idealistic young man expounded, "it seems to me the world is crazy. The rich, who have lots of money, buy on credit, but the poor, who don't have a cent, must pay cash. Don't you think it should be the other way around? The rich, having money, should pay cash; and the poor, having none, should get credit."

The grocer smiled at his son's lack of business acumen. "But," he pointed out, "if a storekeeper gave credit to the poor, he himself would soon become poor."

"So what?" countered the college boy. "Then he would be able to buy on credit, too!"

AN IMAGINATIVE EXECUTIVE of a New York credit service sent the following letter to one of his delinquent accounts:

"Dear Sir:

"After checking our files, we note that we have done more for you than your mother did— we've carried you for 15 months!"

# BUREAUCRACY

MOISHE AND BECKY went to City Hall to apply for a wedding license. They were directed to the third floor where they had to fill out forms. When that was done, they were to take the forms to the sixth floor, pay a fee, and then they'd get their license.

They obediently filled out the forms, went up to the sixth floor and waited on a line. Eventually, they came to the front of the line, where the man looked over the forms.

"Becky?" he said. "Your legal name isn't Becky, is it? Go back to the third floor and fill out a new form with your real name, Rebecca."

So the couple went back downstairs, filled out another form, returned to the sixth floor, waited on line, and arrived before the man again.

This time the man got up to the part with Moishe's name on it. He frowned, "Moishe? That doesn't sound like an English name to me."

"Well, my real name is Michael," said Moishe, "but I've always been called Moishe—"

"Go back down to the third floor," interrupted the man, "and fill these forms out in English!"

So the couple went down again, filled out another form, came back up to the sixth floor, waited again on line, and eventually arrived at the window. The names were okay this time, but this time the man found the address unacceptable. They had written 'Williamsburg, New York.' "Williamsburg is just a section of Brooklyn," said the man. "Go downstairs and rewrite the forms, and this time write 'Brooklyn, New York' instead of 'Williamsburg, New York.'"

Moishe and Becky went through the whole procedure yet another time and returned to the sixth floor. Finally, after several hours at City Hall, everything seemed in order.

Moishe sighed and turned to Becky. "It's worth it, sweetheart. Now our little boy will know that everything is legal."

The official glared at them. "Did I hear you

say you have a little boy?" Moishe admitted they did.

"You already have a baby and you're just getting a wedding license today? Do you know that makes your little boy a technical bastard?"

Moishe was icy. "So?" he countered. "That's what the man on the third floor said *you* are, and *you* seem to be doing all right!"

The head of one Washington administration was approached by his secretary. "Sir," she said, "our files are becoming overcrowded."

"What do you suggest we do?" asked the busy administrator.

"I think we ought to destroy all correspondence more than six years old," answered the secretary.

"By all means," the prudent bureaucrat responded, "go right ahead. But be sure to make copies."

THE LICENSE BUREAU CLERK, checking over the applicant's papers, was astounded to note that the man had filled in the spaces, "Age of Father, if living" 105, and "Age of Mother, if living" 102.

The surprised clerk surveyed the middle aged man. "Are your parents really that old?" he asked.

"No," was the reply, "but they would be if living."

ALL OF AMERICA'S CITIES have problems with air pollution, and St. Louis created a Smoke Inspector to deal with its problem.

Unfortunately, it was an appointed position. Thus the job often fell to those people who were politically deserving, instead of to those who were qualified to handle pollution problems. Many men who took the post expected a large salary for very little work.

One not-too-bright appointee, selected some years ago, was irritated that he had to submit reports on his progress from time to time. Calling in his secretary at the end of the first month of his tenure, he dictated the following report:

"From the office of the Smoke Inspector. Have inspected the smoke of St. Louis for the month of December and have found it to be of good quality."

# BUSINESS

The week after Labor Day, Abe Cohen and Nat Goldfarb met for lunch. They hadn't seen each other for several months. As they sat down, Abe began complaining.

"Nat, my friend, I have just lived through a summer the likes of which I never thought I would see. June was already a disaster. Never in my entire business career have I seen a June like that. Yet when July came I realized that June had been quite good, for with July I went down through the floor and into the sub-basement. July was absolutely unbelievable and indescribable, and when I tell you—"

But at this point Nat interrupted impatiently. "For heaven's sake, Abie, why are you coming to me with these piddling matters?" he said, even more depressed than his friend. "If you want a tale of *real* trouble, here it is. Yesterday my son, my only son, on whom I had been placing all my hopes, came to me and told me he was getting married to another boy. Do you hear me? My son has become an open homosexual! What can be worse than *that*?"

"I'll tell you," Nat answered, "August!"

Two garment manufacturers met in the bank one Friday morning.

"So, Stanley," said one, "how's business?"

The other man just shrugged. "Ehhh," he said.

The first one smiled. "Well, for this time of the year, that's not bad!"

SAMMY FELL VICTIM to inflation and found he had to give up his business. After a while, he didn't even have money left for food, and was reduced to begging in the streets.

A businessman walked down the street, and Sammy decided he might be the generous sort. So he approached the man and said, "Sir, can you spare three cents for a cup of coffee?"

The man looked surprised. "Where can you get a cup of coffee for three cents?" he asked.

"What do you mean 'where?'" Sammy scoffed. "Who buys retail?"

Moe met Sammy for a glass of tea.
"So how's business?" asked Sammy.
"Fine," said Moe, "except for one thing."
"And what is that?"
"It's rotten."



A young man recently graduated from Yale took a job with a large clothing firm as a stockroom boy. He worked hard, and within a few months was made a salesman. In another six months he was promoted to sales manager, and soon afterwards to general manager.

A few days after his last promotion, he was called into the president's office. The president explained that he would retire soon and turn his position over to the young man.

The young man said, "Thanks."

"Thanks!" roared the president. "You've been with this firm only a year and already you're taking over the presidency. Is that all you can think of to say?"

"Well," amended the young man, "thanks a lot, Dad."



The prospect of following in his father's footsteps and becoming a poor farmer did not appeal to young Smith. So, he acted quickly when the job of sexton at the local church fell vacant and was first in line with his application. But the minister was forced to refuse him, for the fact was Smith could neither read nor write.

Smith moved to the city, found a job, and invested wisely. By the time he reached 40, he had become a multi-millionaire.

When Smith returned to his home town, it came as a shock to everyone that the prosperous businessman still could neither read nor write.

"It is amazing, Mr. Smith," an old friend said to him, "that you have accomplished so much without being able to read or write. Can you imagine what you would be today if you could?"

"Certainly," Smith chuckled. "A church sexton."

The bald headed barber was trying to sell his customer a bottle of hair tonic.

"But how can you sell this stuff when you yourself are bald!" challenged the customer.

"Nothing wrong with that!" came the reply. "There are 10,000 guys selling brassieres!"

THE YOUNG SON of a garment maker was in school one day when the teacher asked him to name the four seasons.

The boy stood up and said, "I only know two: busy and slack!"

THE PRESIDENT of the congregation had to undergo surgery. The board met to decide how to show their concern. Finally, it was agreed that the secretary of the congregation would visit the president in the hospital.

Two days after the operation, the secretary visited the sickroom. "I bring you the good wishes of our board," he said. "We hope you get well and live to be 120 years old!"

The president smiled back weakly.

"And that's an official resolution," continued the secretary, "passed by a vote of twelve to nine."

TWO PEDDLERS WERE standing in the street talking. They had plenty of time to talk because they had very little business.

One said, "You know, if I had Rockefeller's

money, I'd be even richer than Rockefeller."

"What!" cried the other man, "How could that be?"

"Because," explained the first, "I'd have all of Rockefeller's money besides what I make from the pushcart "

Danny was an inveterate bargain hunter. He hadn't a penny to his name, but whenever he saw a bargain he couldn't resist it.

One day a friend of his came to see him. Jim said, "Danny, I've got a terrific bargain for you. A boatload has arrived for the Barnum and Bailey Circus and they have an overstock. They've got an elephant on board, a baby elephant, that's worth at least $2,000 and I can land it for you for only $300."

Danny looked at Jim as if he were half crazy. "What! An elephant! An elephant in my one-room apartment? You must be out of your mind! In the first place, there's no room for it. And in the second place, how could I feed it? In the third place, what could I do with it? Don't be nuts!"

"But," persisted Jim, "I'm telling you this elephant is worth 2,000 bucks and I can get it for you for a mere 300, maybe even for 250."

Danny was adamant. "Get the hell out of here, will you? You're off your rocker. I don't need an elephant. I don't want an elephant. Leave me alone with elephants."

But Jim knew his friend and he continued hammering away. "Listen, Danny," he said, "the fact is they have an overstock. You know, I think if I put it to 'em I could get you two elephants for the same 200 bucks."

"Now you're talkin'," said Danny.


A MERCHANT MOVED DOWN SOUTH from New York into one of the backwater towns. He seemed to be doing rather well, but then at about the beginning of April, the sales started to slacken very noticeably.

Sam Cohen pondered and pondered about the cause of the decline in business. Suddenly he realized, as he walked the streets, that every other establishment on Main Street had an Easter sign out front and that all the windows were especially dressed for the holiday.

Sam was in a quandary. He was a religious Jew—how could he, in good conscience, pay obeisance to Easter? He was up all night thinking. The next morning he arose and his face was beaming. He had worked out the solution.

That afternoon, Cohen's general store also contained an Easter sign. It read: "Christ is risen, but Cohen's prices are still the same."

"How is business?" asked Mike, as he walked into his friend's dress shop.

"Terrible," complained Jim. "Business stinks. Yesterday I only sold one dress, and today it's even worse."

"And how could it be worse?" asked Mike.

"How could it be worse?" wailed Jim. "Today the customer returned the dress she bought yesterday."

WELL-TO-DO FINANCIER Otto H. Kahn was being driven through New York one day when he passed a storefront sign reading: "Abram Cahn. Cousin of Otto H. Kahn."

The banker was furious at the misrepresentation and had his lawyer call the store immediately and threaten proceedings if the sign was not removed.

A few days later, Kahn asked his chauffeur to drive him past the store again, to see if the man had kept his promise. Sure enough, the old sign was gone. In its place was a new sign, which read: "Abram Cahn. *Formerly* cousin of Otto H. Kahn."

A GROCER HAD SUFFERED a heart attack and was carried upstairs to his apartment. Now, pale and weak, he knew there was no hope. The doctor said it would be only a matter of minutes.

"Are you there, Molly?" asked the man softly. His sorrowful wife pressed his hand.

"And Bernard, are you there?" he went on faintly.

"Yes, father," came his son's reply.

"And Marsha, you're there?"

"Yes, father," wept his daughter.

Then the grocer's voice came out full force. "You're all here, so who's minding the store?" he growled.

BUSINESS WAS SO TERRIBLE in the garment district that Horowitz decided he couldn't take it any more. He was facing bankruptcy and utter shame and ruin. Suicide was the only way out.

Taking the elevator from his sixth-floor office all the way up to the twenty-fourth floor, Horowitz said a mental good-bye to his wife and his business partner Finkel. Then he jumped.

As he fell past the fifteenth floor, he overheard the chairman of Macy's talking on the phone. "We'll be looking for a lot of soft textured clothing next fall," he heard the chairman say.

As Horowitz passed his own office on the sixth floor, he yelled to his partner, "Finkel! Cut velvet! Cut velvet!"

THE PRESIDENT and chairman of the board of one of the nation's largest corporations was conducting an annual meeting of the stockholders. He presented the board's officers to the gathering and then began the meeting's business.

"Wait a minute," shouted a voice from the audience. "Who are you and what do you do for this company?"

The president was surprised, but he remained composed. "I'm your chairman," he said clamly. "And, of course, you know the duties of a chairman. I'd say he was roughly the equivalent of parsley on a platter of fish."

Morris had just started his new job as a bus driver and he approached his work conscientiously. For five straight days, his fares totaled a steady $75. No matter how diligent he was, he always ended the day with the same $75.

The following Monday, however, Morris proudly handed the company cashier a pouch containing $314. The bus official was astonished. "Fantastic!" he said. "How did you do it?"

"It was easy," explained Morris. "After five days on that cockamamy route, I figured business would *never* improve. So I drove over to 14th Street, and worked there. I tell you, that street is a gold mine!"

SAM WEINSTEIN AND Sol Applebaum owned a clothing factory and were quite pleased with the way business was going. One day, Sam decided that a well-to-do person ought to have a more elegant name. So he started calling himself Whittaker. And he changed the sign on the front of the factory from WEINSTEIN AND APPLEBAUM to WHITTAKER AND APPLEBAUM.

Sol was not to be outdone. He wanted to be elegant, too. So he also changed his name to Whittaker. Now the sign in front of the factory read WHITTAKER AND WHITTAKER.

One morning, a prospective buyer came to call. "I'd like to see Mr. Whittaker," the man had said.

"Which one?" answered the receptionist, "Weinstein or Applebaum?"

# BUSINESS & SEX

The boss had been after his secretary for almost a year. He had been suggesting all kinds of things to her. On this particular evening, he was unusually persistent.

"Oh, come on," he said, "let's go out and have supper, then go to the theatre, then to a nightclub and then you will come up to my apartment."

The blonde clipped back, "I'd like you to comprehend that I am adamant and didactic in my refusal of your salacious, mendacious, and denigrating proposition."

The boss said, "I don't get it!"

The secretary answered, "That's just what I have been trying to tell you."

BOTH PARTNERS IN a clothing shop had been having an affair with Sally, the salesgirl, and both were shocked to learn that the young lady was pregnant. Each tried to lay the blame on the other.

Finally one of the partners went on a business trip, and while he was away young Sally was confined. Soon after, the partner on the road received a telegram from his associate: "Sally gave birth to twins. Mine died!"

A forward young secretary went to a Miami convention with her boss. At the hotel desk, the gentleman was informed that, due to the convention, only one room was available. He reluctantly agreed to share it with his secretary.

In the elevator, the businessman sternly warned his secretary that once they got in the room she was to keep her mind strictly on business. The girl agreed.

But that night, after the lights had been turned out, the secretary decided on a little fun.

"Yoo, hoo, Mr. Wright," she cooed.

"What is it?" growled her boss.

"Can I have another blanket? I'm awfully chilly."

The boss angrily brought her one of his blankets. After another minute of silence, the young lady cooed again. "Mr. Wright, yooo-hooo."

"Now what is it?"

"Would you get me a glass of water? I'm very thirsty."

There was a slight pause. Then the businessman whispered, "Miss Smith, how would you like to be Mrs. Wright for just tonight?"

"Oh, I'd just love that!" came the reply.

"All right," he bellowed, "then go and get your own glass of water!"


AFTER BARGAINING FOR HOURS, Witherspoon and his client finally approached an agreement. Witherspoon studied the client's latest offer, then pressed the intercom to talk to the bookkeeper. "Miss Holly," he yelled, pencil poised in hand, "if someone offered you $6,000 less 8%, how much would you take off?"

The voice came back immediately: "Everything but my earrings!"

# BUSINESS PARTNERS

THE DEBATING SOCIETY was discussing ethics, and it was MacDougal's turn to express his views.

"I'll give you my view, gentlemen, with an example," he began. "Let's say a man came into my store to buy something, and after he left I discovered that he gave me a ten dollar bill instead of a five. Now, the ethical question is: Should I or should I not tell my partner?"

FINKEL SPENT ALL MORNING trying to contact Saperstein and Shapiro, an important account. But when he asked for Saperstein, the secretary told him the man was out. And when he asked for Shapiro, the secretary told him he was tied up.

He'd called back five times, when he'd finally had enough. "What kind of business is this?" he fumed at the secretary. "One partner's out all morning, and the other's tied up for hours on end. What's going on there?"

The secretary apologized. "I'm sorry, Mr. Finkel, but, you see, whenever Mr. Saperstein goes out, he ties Mr. Shapiro up."

Two BUSINESS PARTNERS had never had an argument in 20 years. One week one of the pair came down with a virus and missed a few days at the store.

On the fourth day of his absence the ailing partner received a call from his associate, who told him, "I just found $15,000 missing from the safe. What should I do?"

His partner replied quickly, "Put it back!"

Two PARTNERS IN THE GARMENT industry were having business problems; it looked as if they might have to declare bankruptcy. But at the brink, a particular line of dresses seemed to lure a buyer. A West Coast outlet wanted to buy the whole line, at a price which would put the partners well into the black. The partners were overjoyed.

"The only thing is," warned the buyer, "I have to have the deal approved by the home office. I'm sure they'll agree, but I do have to check with them. I'm going back tomorrow. If you don't hear from me by Friday closing time, you can be sure everything's okay."

The week went by slowly; and Friday crawled. The two men sat without moving at their desks, unable to concentrate on any kind of work. Without this deal, they would definitely go under. They sweated the hours out, minute by minute.

Two o'clock went by, three o'clock, then four o'clock, and now they were close to pay dirt. Four-thirty came, and they were holding their breath. Suddenly, a messenger burst into the office. "Telegram!" he said. The men froze in terror.

Finally, one of the partners stood up. Slowly he opened the telegram, and read it quickly.

Then came a shriek of joy. "Harry! Good news! Your brother died!"

# COURTING & SEDUCTION

Nate and Becky were spending a Sunday at the amusement park. They were having a lovely time. Then Nate decided to buy tickets for the tunnel of love.

The ride was slow and pleasant. When they emerged into the light, Becky smoothed down her dress, dabbed on her lipstick, and smiled shyly at Nate. She said demurely, "Nate, you know, you shouldn't have did it."

Nate turned to her and insisted: "I *didn't* did it."

Becky was flabbergasted. "What! *You* didn't did it? Well then, who *did* did it?"

In the midst of a furious downpour, a young lady pulled up at a motel to spend the night. "I'm sorry," the hotel clerk told her, "but we don't have another empty room. I just rented the last room, a double, to that young man over there."

The lady, realizing that this was the only motel within miles, approached the young man: "The clerk told me that you just rented the last room," she said. "I have nowhere to stay tonight and it's raining too hard to drive. You don't know anybody that I know, and I don't know anybody that you know, so would you mind if I occupied one of the beds in your room?"

The young man agreed.

That night, when they had climbed into separate beds and turned out the light, the lady said, "It's kind of cold near the window here, and your bed is wide enough for two. You don't know anybody that I know, and I don't know anybody that you know, so would you mind if I moved over into your bed with you?"

The young man said he had no objection.

A few minutes later, the young lady spoke again. "You don't know anybody that I know, and I don't know anybody that you know, so how about having a party?"

The young man shrugged. "If you don't know anybody that I know, and I don't know anybody that you know," he said, "then who can we invite?"

Women often react negatively to compliments given on the street, but one gentleman knew how to handle the situation.

The lady who caught his eye was window-shopping. He trailed her for several blocks, waiting for the right moment to speak.

But before he could do so, she noticed him and became annoyed. Impatiently, she walked up to him and said, "You've been following me for three blocks. I saw you. You can stop right now. I'm not the type of girl you can pick up."

Thinking quickly, the gentlemen offered, "Madame, I am not picking you up. I am picking you *out*."

By the time they parted, she agreed to a date with a smile.

Stanley was already in his twenties and he had never had a date with a girl, so his older brother decided it was time to do something about it. He arranged a blind date for Stanley with a nice young girl who was just as innocent as Stanley. But Stanley was very nervous. His hands became clammy and his tongue felt stiff as marble.

"Help me, Mark. I don't know how to talk to girls. How can I be a good conversationalist like you?" asked Stanley.

Mark had some advice to offer. "Listen, Stan," he said, "I have a formula that never fails. Talk about family, food, and philosophy. Any of those topics is guaranteed to get a girl talking. Try it! I'm sure it'll work."

So Stanley went to meet the girl. She was pretty and shy. Stanley wanted very much to make a good impression. He thought of his brother's advice. First, he'd talk family.

"Tell me," he began nervously, "do you have a brother?"

"No!" came the girl's swift reply.

"Oh." Stanley was stymied, so he moved to the topic of food. "Do you like noodles?"

"No!" she said again.

But Stanley wasn't at a loss. He remembered his brother's advice. He'd talk philosophy. "Say," he said, "if you had a brother, would he like noodles?"


TWO CHUMS WERE HAVING a private little conversation. "Do you know," said one, "I'm amazed at how popular I am, and I cannot for the life of me understand why the men cluster around me. Tell me the truth, Jane, is it my complexion?"

"No," said Jane.

"Well, do you think it's my figure?"

"No," came the reply.

"Well, is it my personality?"

"No, not really."

"Well, I give up."

"Uh, huh!" exclaimed the other, "Now you got it!"

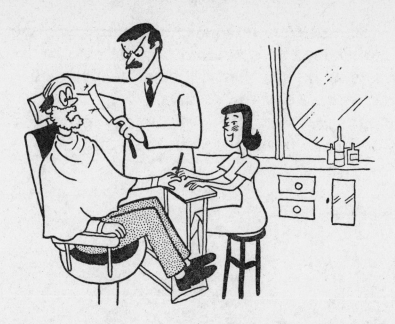

Stopping in an unfamiliar barber shop for a shave, a young playboy took a fancy to the manicure girl and suggested dinner and a show that evening.

"I don't think I ought to," the girl demurred. "I'm married."

"Why don't you ask your husband," the playboy suggested. "I'm sure he wouldn't object."

"You can ask him yourself," the girl shrugged. "He's shaving you."

THIS STORY CONCERNS a particularly persistent suitor. He lived in Chicago and courted a girl in Oshkosh for two years.

Things somehow went wrong and she wouldn't see him any longer. So he took to the mails and he sent her a special delivery letter three times a day for 33 days.

On the 34th day, his strategy produced results. The girl eloped with the mailman.

A YOUNG FELLOW brought home his bride-to-be to be appraised by his father.

The older man was flabbergasted, chagrined, and embarrassed. He took the boy aside into the next room and whispered in his ear, "I never saw such a homely girl. She's got hair on her chin; her eyes are watching each other; and her teeth are crooked."

"Pop, you don't have to whisper," the son replied. "You can talk louder. She's deaf too."

THE IMPASSIONED SUITOR bent close to his escort and whispered in her ear, "Say the three little words that will make me walk on air."

The young lady smiled sweetly and told him, "Go hang yourself."

A young wolf took his date for a drive along a lonely country road. They'd reached a quiet spot when the car suddenly stopped.

"I guess we're out of gas," he grinned.

The girl immediately opened her handbag and pulled out a large bottle.

"Hey!" the wolf exclaimed. "You've got a whole fifth there! What kind is it?"

"Gulf regular," the girl replied.

# CUSTOMERS

Mrs. Kohansky went to her butcher of many years and said, "Bernie, today I need a beautiful chicken, maybe four pounds."

Bernie pointed out three chickens in the display counter, but Mrs. Kohansky turned up her nose at all of them. "I asked for a *beautiful* chicken," she sniffed.

So Bernie went to the back of the store, and from his refrigerator room he extracted an especially plump fowl. He brought it forward with pride.

The lady was cautious. She took the chicken and slowly began to examine each part with her fingers—lifting the wings, feeling the breast, and groping inside the cavity.

Finally, the butcher's patience waned. "Tell me, Mrs. Kohansky," he demanded, "do you think *you* could pass such a test?"

A suburban lady entered an exclusive boutique to look for a hat. She tried on many, but none seemed to satisfy her. One was too large, one too wide, another too dressy.

Finally, the exasperated saleslady said sweetly to her, "I wish I had a dozen like you," and walked to the back of the store.

Another saleslady, who had overheard the remark, was puzzled. "Why on earth did you say that to that obnoxious customer?"

"Because," said the worn-out woman through gritted teeth, "I have a hundred like her, but I wish I had only a dozen!"

IT WAS A BROILING day in July. Mrs. Finkelstein went into a store to buy a fan.

"What kind fan do you want?" asked Levy, the storekeeper. "We have fans for a nickel, for a quarter, and for a dollar."

"So give me one for a nickel," said Mrs. Finkelstein.

"O.K." said Levy, as he handed her a thin Japanese paper fan.

In 10 minutes, Mrs. Finkelstein was back. "Look what trash you sold me!" she shouted. "The fan broke."

"It did?" said Levy. "And how did you use it?"

"How did I use it?" replied Mrs. Finkelstein. "How do you use a fan? I held it in my hand, and I waved it back and forth in front of my face. Did you ever?"

"Oh no!" explained Levy, "With a five-cent fan, you got to hold it still, in both hands, like this, and wave your head back and forth in front of it."

A bearded old Jew entered a delicatessen and pointed to a slab of ham behind the glass counter. "A quarter pound of the corned beef, if you please."

The counter man noticed the beard and thought it his duty to inform the old man. "I'm sorry, sir," he said quietly, "but that's ham!"

"And who asked you?" retorted the elder.

Sadie Weintraub asked for two bagels.

"That'll be twenty cents, please," said the baker.

"Twenty cents!" exclaimed Sadie. "Why,

that's ten cents a bagel! The man across the street only charges *six* cents!"

"So, buy them across the street," shrugged the baker.

"But they're all out of bagels across the street," said Sadie.

"Lady, when I'm all out of bagels, I only charge a nickel apiece."

A man walked into a very expensive bakery shop where they made cakes to order.

"I'd like you to bake me a cake in the shape of the letter S," he said. "Can you do that?"

"Why certainly!" said the baker. "We can make a cake in any shape at all. When would you like it to be ready?"

"Have it ready by three o'clock tomorrow. I'll call for it," said the man.

The next day at three o'clock, the man came in for his cake. The baker proudly displayed the cake he had made. It was shaped like the letter S and decorated beautifully.

"Oh!" cried the man. "That's all wrong! That's not what I want. You made it in the shape of a regular printed S. I wanted a graceful *script* S. That won't do at all!"

"I'm terribly sorry you're so disappointed," said the baker. "We aim to please. I'll make you another cake at no extra charge. Don't worry."

"All right then," said the man. "I'll be back at six o'clock for the cake. And this time I hope it's right."

At six o'clock the man came in. The baker brought in the new cake. He was all smiles. "Isn't this a beauty!" he exclaimed.

The man looked at the cake. His face lit up.

"That's perfect!" he said. "Just what I wanted."

"I'm delighted," said the baker. "Now tell me, Sir, what kind of a box shall I put it in?"

"Oh, don't bother wrapping it up," said the man. "I'll eat it here."

# DINNER PARTIES

On UNFORTUNATE HOST found himself suffering
the boorishness of a particularly uncouth guest.
The fellow had been increasingly boisterous
throughout the cocktail hour, and reached a
zenith of rudeness at the dinner table.

At one point, the dimwit speared some meat
from his plate and held it up to the rest of the
guests. Flushed with self-importance, he addressed his host. "Is this *pig?*" he asked.

The host controlled his anger and quietly
said, "To which end of the fork do you refer?"

Almost in awe of the well-known orator Daniel
Webster, one nineteenth-century congressional
wife pulled out all the stops in preparing a
sumptuous repast when he came to dinner. She
heaped his plate high with food, and when he
emptied it, she piled on more.

Webster, however, could not stuff himself
past his limit, and finally gave up. The matron
began to pout.

"You're hardly eating a thing, Mr. Webster,"

she worried. "Can it be that something displeases you? Won't you have just a little bit more?"

After a fair amount of such fussing, Webster spoke gently but firmly. "Madam," he said, "permit me to assure you that I sometimes eat more than at other times, but never less."

Most people feel embarrassed when making excuses to avoid an invitation. But John Barrymore was a well-known actor and therefore felt he could be blunt.

A major film producer was once giving a party and, impressed with his importance, he had an assistant telephone the guests.

When Barrymore answered the phone, he was told, "I am speaking for Mr. Laskwyn, who wants you to attend an important party he is giving tommorrow."

Barrymore assumed his best voice and replied, "And I am speaking for John Barrymore, who has a previous engagement which he will make as soon as you have hung up."

THE MACGREGORS of Scotland were all big, husky, country men. They knew the wilds of their own surroundings, but had little use for the finer aspects of civilization. When a problem arose with respect to their land rights, the head of the clan—known as The MacGregor—sent to the university in Edinburgh for an attorney.

The city lawyer was pale and slight next to the clansmen, but he had the expertise they needed, so he was generously thanked and invited to share the MacGregors' gargantuan dinner. Entering the huge dining hall, the lawyer was pointed to one end of the table overflowing with food.

The lawyer, not wanting to usurp the master's place at the head of the table, said, "Oh, sir, I could not sit in the chair of The MacGregor himself."

"You may sit," The MacGregor assured him, "since it is he himself who invites you to do so."

Looking around at the tall sons beside him, the lawyer backed off further. "Only The MacGregor should sit at the head of the table," he said.

The MacGregor laughed heartily and clapped the attorney on the back. "Sit where you are told, you foolish little man, for wherever The MacGregor sits, *there* is the head of the table."

# DIVORCE

The divorce-court judge listened intently as the distraught wife charged. her husband with nonsupport.

After her testimony, the judge told the husband: "You obviously haven't taken proper care of this good woman, and I'm going to give her $25 a month."

The husband beamed with delight. "Why that's mighty nice of you, Your Honor," he said, "and I'll give her a dollar or two from time to time myself."

THE WIFE WAS pleading her case before the divorce court judge. "All I'm asking, Your Honor, is that my husband leave me the way he found me."

"But lady," the judge replied, "that's impossible."

"Why impossible?" she persisted. "He found me a widow!"

# DOCTORS & MEDICINE

The poor tailor was beside himself. His wife was sick and perhaps dying. He called on the only doctor nearby.

"Please, save my wife, doctor! I'll pay anything!"

"But what if I can't cure her?" asked the doctor.

"I'll pay whether you cure her or kill her, if only you'll come right away!"

So the doctor promptly visited the woman, but within a week, she died. Soon a bill arrived charging the tailor a tremendous fee. The tailor couldn't hope to pay, so he asked the doctor to appear with him before the local rabbi to arbit-rate the case.

"He agreed to pay me for treating his wife," stated the physician, "whether I cured her or killed her."

The rabbi was thoughtful. "Well, did you cure her?" he asked.

"No," admitted the doctor.

"And did you kill her?"

"I certainly did not!" expostulated the physician.

"In that case," the rabbi said with finality, "you have no grounds on which to base a fee."


Mr. Carson placed a frantic phone call to his doctor and explained that his wife, who always slept with her mouth open, had a mouse caught in her throat.

"I'll be over in a few minutes," said the doctor. "In the meantime, try waving a piece of cheese in front of her mouth."

When the doctor reached the Carson apartment, he found Mr. Carson waving a five-pound haddock in front of his wife's face.

"What are you doing?" exclaimed the doctor. "I told you to wave a piece of cheese. Mice don't like haddock."

"I know," Mr. Carson gasped, "But I've got to get the cat out first."

A group of Peace Corps volunteers were being briefed before leaving for a remote African country.

"Now, boys," the instructor told them, "you may very well run across some poisonous snakes where you're going, and one of you could be bitten. Let me say, first of all, that no matter what you've heard, drinking whiskey is no antidote. If you're bitten by a snake, you must make a cut near the bite so that it bleeds freely. Then put your mouth over the gash, and suck out as much blood as you can."

"But, sir," one recruit called out, "suppose you're bitten on the backside?"

The instructor stared back and cracked a grin. "Then, my boy, you'll find out who your friends are."

THE AMBASSADOR'S WIFE was walking to a luncheon one day when she noticed an accident that had occurred at the street corner ahead. Suddenly, she was grateful for the first-aid course she'd recently attended.

As she told her husband later, "I was crossing the street when I saw the poor man lying there. He had been hit by a cab and was in a bad way.

"Then all my first aid came back to me, and I stooped right down and put my head between my knees to keep from fainting."

A MAN CAME to a doctor complaining that he had an uncontrollable cough. The doctor gave him a bottle of castor oil and said, "Go home and drink down the entire bottle, and come back tomorrow."

When the patient came back next day, the doctor asked, "Did you take the castor oil?"

The man answered "Yes." The doctor then continued, "Do you still cough?"

The patient said, "Yes, I continue to cough."

The doctor gave him a second bottle of castor oil and said, "Take this, and come back tomorrow."

The next day, the man returned. The doctor asked him, "Do you still cough?"

And the patient said, "Yes, I still cough regularly."

The doctor then gave him yet another bottle of castor oil and said, "Drink this entire bottle tonight and come back tomorrow morning."

The patient returned, and the doctor looked at the poor wretch and said, "Do you cough now?"

The patient quiveringly answered, "I don't cough anymore—I'm afraid to."


"Now TELL ME," said the Doctor, "do you always stutter?"

The patient thought for a while and then said, "N-n-no d-d-doc. J-j-just when I t-t-talk!"

"Doctor, I feel terrible," the staid businessman told his doctor. "Tell me what's wrong with me."

"First let me ask you a few questions," the doctor replied. "Do you drink much alcohol?"

"I have never touched the stuff in my life," the businessman replied indignantly.

"Do you smoke?" the doctor continued.

"I have never touched the filthy weed in my life."

"Do you stay up late at night?"

"Of course not!" the patient huffed. "I'm in bed every night by ten-thirty for a good night's rest."

"Well then," the doctor continued, "do you have sharp pains in the head?"

"Exactly!" the businessman replied. "I have pains in the head all the time."

"Just as I suspected," the doctor smirked. "Your halo is on too tight!"


A worried, middle-aged businessman went to visit his doctor. He wanted advice on how to live to be one hundred.

"Well," said the doctor, "you'll have to give up smoking, drinking, and women."

"Will that make me live to be one hundred?" inquired the businessman.

"No," said the doctor, "but it will make it seem like it."

A LOVELY BUT rather flat-chested young woman visited a physician for her periodic physical examination.

"Please remove your blouse," the doctor told her.

"Oh, no," the young lady protested, "I just couldn't!"

"Come, come," the doctor replied, "let's not make mountains out of molehills."

SIMPSON, BOTHERED BY a sore throat, went to his doctor for a prescription. The doctor's pretty nurse answered the bell.

"Is the doctor in?" Simpson asked in a hoarse whisper.

"No, come in!" the young lady whispered back.

A PATIENT WAS MAKING his first visit to the doctor.

"And whom did you consult about your illness before you came to me?" the doctor inquired.

"Only the druggist down at the corner," replied the patient.

The doctor did not conceal his contempt for the medical advice of people not qualified to practice medicine.

"And what sort of ridiculous advice did that fool give you?"

"He told me," replied the patient innocently, "to see you."


THE NURSE at the front desk answered the telephone. "Hello. Can I help you?"

"Oh, nurse," came the voice, "can you please tell me how Sol Weinstein is doing?"

The nurse was kind. "Of course," she said, "just one moment while I get out his chart. . . . Well, it seems he's doing just fine! The doctor has written here that he can be released on Friday!"

"Oh, that's wonderful!" said the voice.

"And who can I tell him called?" asked the nurse.

"It's me! Weinstein!" said the voice. "I decided to phone you because the doctor won't tell me anything!"

ONE DAY, A BUTCHER accidentally cut his throat while shaving. The bleeding was so profuse, he fainted. He was carted off to the hospital.

When the butcher awoke, the nurse told him what had happened, and informed him that he wouldn't be able to eat for a while. But all he wanted to know was what his hospital stay would cost him. The nurse told him he was being charged $150 a day.

The man was furious that he had to pay so much and he wasn't even allowed to eat. He wanted his money's worth! So he demanded a glass of tea.

The nurse quietly went down the hall and got him a cup of tea. Then she returned and calmly injected the tea into the tube attached to the butcher's arm.

"Oy, Oy, Oy!" came the shouts.

"What's the matter?" the nurse asked. "Is the tea too hot?"

"No," yelled the butcher, "It's too sweet. How can I drink tea without lemon!"


Two LADIES LAY side by side on chaise lounges poolside at a swank Miami Beach hotel. One couldn't stop talking about her analyst. The other just lay prone and listened.

Finally, the listener entered the competition. "You ought to try *my* doctor. He's marvelous!"

Her companion asked, "Why should I see your doctor? There's nothing wrong with me."

"Oh!" replied the other, "My doctor's wonderful, he'll *find* something!"

"TELL ME THE TRUTH," the sick man told his doctor. "I want to know just how ill I am."

"Well," said the doctor, "you are very sick—very low. In fact, I feel that I should ask you if there is anyone you would like to see."

"Yes," murmured the patient feebly.

"Who is it?"

"Another doctor."

A woman called up a doctor's office and said to the nurse, "I'm missing my panties. I just wonder if I left them in the dressing room."

The nurse said she'd look, but came back in a

moment and said, "I'm sorry, madam, but your panties are not here."

"Oh, well then, never mind," answered the other. "I must have left them at the dentist's."

SADIE WASN'T FEELING WELL, and she knew she should see a doctor. So she asked her friend Becky the name of the doctor she used.

"His name's Feinstein," said Becky, "but you should know he's expensive."

"How expensive?" asked Sadie.

"Well, it's fifty dollars for the first visit, and twenty-five for every visit after that."

So Sadie went off to see Dr. Feinstein. When her turn came to be examined, she smiled brightly and said to the nurse, "Hi, honey. Here I am again!"

AN OLD LADY went to her physician and complained of constipation. The doctor asked, "Do you do anything about it?"

"Of course I do, doctor. I sit on the toilet for three hours every day."

"No, no, I don't mean that, Mrs. Jones. I mean do you take anything?"

"Of course, doctor. I take along my knitting."

AN 82-YEAR-OLD woman tottered into Dr. Meyrowitz's office. "Doctor," she told her physician, "I'm not feeling too good."

"I'm sorry, Mrs. Kupnick, some things not even modern medicine can cure. I can't make you any younger, you know."

Mrs. Kupnick replied, "Doctor, who asked you to make me younger? All I want is for you to make me older.

"I GOT INSOMNIA real bad," complained a man to his doctor.

"Insomnia," said the doctor, "is insomnia. How bad can it be? What do you mean, 'real bad insomnia'?"

"Well," said the patient, "I got it real bad. I can't even sleep when it's time to get up!"

MRS. MOSKOWITZ was aging. She had passed 81 and was having some "woman trouble." Upon the advice of her daughter, she went to visit a gynecologist. She remained quiet throughout the examination, but when it was over she turned to Dr. Lipsky.

"Dr. Lipsky," she said, "you seem to be such a nice young man. Tell me, does your mother know how you're making a living?"

A MAN LAY IN BED in a hospital ward. Three doctors approached him and asked him what he was in the hospital for. The patient replied that he wanted to be castrated. The doctors looked at him askance, and said in unison, "What!"

He repeated: "Yes, I want to be castrated."

The operation was performed. After a few days, the patient was dressed and on his way out of the hospital when he passed the maternity ward, and saw a small crowd gathered in a room. He asked the nurse what was going on. "Oh," she said, "A little baby boy is being circumcised."

"Circumcised!" he exclaimed "Damn it! That's the word I meant."

# DRINK & BARROOMS

MacDougal, a bear of a man, fell heir to a great fortune. His friends in the saloon were concerned that his sudden wealth would change him, would make him stingy. The boys were discussing the matter, when in dashed MacDougal. He waved them all to the bar. "When MacDougal drinks—everybody drinks!" he shouted.

After all had imbibed, MacDougal slapped a dollar on the bar, and announced: "And when MacDougal pays—everybody pays!"

JACK RAN INTO his friend Freddy on the corner just after Freddy had left a nearby bar. "Listen, Jack," Freddy grinned, "I've got a swell racket for you to try. I just went into that bar and ordered a drink. When the bartender asked for the money I told him I already paid him, and the absent-minded jerk believed me."

Jack immediately walked into the same bar and ordered a martini. The bartender served him and said, "Just a few minutes ago a guy came in here and—"

"What are you yammering to me about?" Tommy interrupted. "Just give me my change."

A study group had been meeting for years, to study the Talmud. One member of the group had a pernicious habit of sipping a little brandy during the meeting. One night he drank just a little more than usual and became quite tipsy.

His companions decided to teach him a lesson. While he was in his drunken stupor, they carried him off to the cemetery and laid him prone among the tombstones.

After awhile, the Talmudic student woke up. He looked about him frightened and aghast. Then he started to reason, "Am I alive? Or am I dead? If I'm alive, what could I be doing here in the graveyard on top of the graves? And if I'm dead, then why do I feel that I must go to the bathroom immediately?"

Sullivan walked into a saloon and ordered a glass of beer. "Say," he called out to the bartender after he'd been served, "how many kegs of beer do you use up every day?"

"Five," answered the proprietor. "Why'd you ask?"

"If I can show you how you can sell twice as much beer, will you buy me a drink?"

"Sure thing," the bartender agreed. "So how can I sell twice as much beer each day?"

"Easy!" said Sullivan. "Fill up the glasses!"

AN ELDERLY SCOTSMAN who was carrying a bottle of whiskey on his hip, slipped and fell on a wee patch of ice on the pavement. As he got up he felt something wet trickling down his leg.

"I hope it's blood," he murmured.

A MAN OBVIOUSLY three sheets to the wind staggered down the street and bumped into a woman of obvious respectability. "You horrible creature," she glowered. "You are the drunkest man I have ever seen."

The drunk turned slowly and said, "Lady, you're the ugliest woman I've ever seen! And that's worse, 'cause when I wake up tomorrow, I'm gonna be sober."

THE ATHLETIC YOUNG MAN was practicing push-ups in the park. A drunk passed by, and stopped to watch for a minute, "Shay, Bud," he slurred, "what happened to your girl?"

The man at the bar innocently turned to the young lady at his left and asked, "Pardon me, miss, do you happen to know the time?"

In a loud voice she replied, *"How dare you make such a proposition to me?"*

The man blushed crimson, aware that every eye in the bar had turned in his direction. He mumbled, "I just asked the time, miss."

In an even louder voice, the young lady screamed, *"If you say one more word I'll call the police!"*

Grabbing his drink, the man hurried to a table at the far end of the room and huddled in a chair, wondering how soon he could sneak out the door.

A few minutes later the young woman joined him at the table. In a quiet voice she told him, "I'm sorry, sir, if I embarrassed you, but I'm a psychology student and I'm writing a thesis on the reaction of men to sudden shocking statements."

The man stared at her for a few seconds, then leaned forward and roared, *"You'll do all that for me for just two dollars?"*

A MINISTER was assailed by a teetotaling preacher for his liberal views about drinking. The minister countered by replying, "There are two drinks mentioned in the Bible: wine: *which gladdeneth the heart of man*, and water: *which quencheth the thirst of the jackasses.*"

Bob entered a bar and ordered a whisky sour, and told the bartender to give the other guy at the bar a drink, too.

Bob's drink arrived, crowned with orange slices and a cherry. When he'd finished his first drink, he called to the bartender, "Fix me another of the same, but forget the fruit."

"Why, you beast!" shrieked the other guy. "I didn't ask for a drink in the first place!"

Two young soldiers had tied one on in a local bar and had lost their way back to their Orlando base. Suddenly one of them bumped into an object in the dark and was knocked off his feet. "Hey, I think we've gotten into a cemetery," he remarked. "Here's a gravestone."

"Whose is it?" asked his buddy.

The soldier lit a match, peered at the stone,

and said, "I don't recognize his name, but he sure lived to an old age—225."

"Wow!" his friend exclaimed. "Who was it?"

The first soldier lit another match. "Some guy named Miles to Miami."

"FIXATION," REMARKED DR. ZEEKEL, a noted psychiatrist, "can be compared to the case of the Montreal drunk who kept muttering, 'It can't be done! It can't be done! It can't be done!' as he stood looking up at a big electric sign that read, 'Drink Canada Dry.'"

The temperance lecturer's voice rose to a fevered pitch as she warned the crowd of the evils of John Barleycorn.

"Who is the richest man in town?" she screamed. "Who has the biggest house? . . . the saloon keeper! Who has the finest clothes? . . . the saloon keeper! And who pays for all this? . . . You do, my friends, you do!"

A few days later, a man who had been in the audience met the lecturer on the street and congratulated her on the rousing speech.

"I'm glad to see that you've given up drinking," the lecturer said.

"Well, not exactly," the man admitted. "I've bought a saloon."

Thompson stared dumbfounded. The well-dressed gentleman next to him at the bar had ordered a vodka martini, had then leaned over the bar and poured the martini in the sink, and had then nibbled away at the rim of the glass. He had not stopped eating the glass until only the stem remained. Then, he had carefully placed the stem in front of him on the bar and then ordered another martini. Five stems were standing before him when he left.

The bartender, noting Thompson's astonishment, winked and said, "You seem surprised, sir."

"I'll say I am," Thompson replied. "That damn fool left the best part."


A WELL-DRESSED GENTLEMAN walked into a tavern, demanded a double shot of scotch, downed it in one gulp, tossed a five-dollar bill on the bar, and walked out without saying a word.

The bartender picked up the bill and put it in his pocket. "How do you like that?" he remarked to the other patrons at the bar. "The guy comes in here, downs a double scotch, leaves a five-dollar tip, and then runs off without paying!"

# EMPLOYMENT OFFICE

A YOUNG MAN was applying for a job in a big company.

"I'm sorry," said the personnel manager, "but the firm is overstaffed; we have more employees now than we really need."

"That's all right," replied the young man, undiscouraged, "the little bit of work I do wouldn't be noticed."

THE DIRECTOR OF A modeling agency was interviewing a young woman for a job. After the usual questions, he ogled her and asked, "Are you a virgin?"

"Yes," she replied coyly, "but I'm not a fanatic about it!"


A watch factory ran an ad for a precision man. The ad offered $100.00 per week. One guy answered the ad, filled out his application and asked for $200.00 a week.

The superintendent asked, "Have you ever worked in a precision factory before?"

The applicant answered, "No."

"And you have the nerve to ask for $200.00 a week?" bellowed the personnel director.

"Of course!" said the jerk, "You know the work is much harder if you don't know how to do it."


YOUNG JAMES CABOT applied for a position with a prestigious firm in Chicago. Since his previous experience had been in Boston, references were requested from his past employer.

The firm in Boston happily complied with information about the Cabots' family background, further supplying data on James' mother's family. All the information indicated Cabot had descended from the finest families in Boston.

The Chicago company wrote back that the information supplied was not really the kind for which they were looking. "We are not contemplating using the young man for breeding purposes," they stated.


A man walked into an employment office to apply for a job. "What's your name?" the clerk asked him.

"Size-Six Halloway," the man replied.

"What kind of name is 'Size-Six'? remarked the clerk.

"That really isn't my name," 'Halloway declared. "As a matter of fact, my name is "Six-And-Seven-Eighths!"

"I don't get you," said the bewildered clerk.

"Well, when I was born my parents didn't know what to name me," he explained, "so they put a few names in a hat. And my father accidentally pulled out the size of the hat."

# GOLF

THE CONFIDENT GOLFER teed up his ball, looked towards the next green, and declared to his caddy, "That's good for one long drive and a putt." He swung violently, topped the ball, and watched it roll a few feet off the tee.

The caddy stepped forward and handed him the putter, smugly muttering, "And now for one hell of a putt!"

Author Bud Kelland and several friends once went to beautiful Echo Lake golf course for a Saturday morning of sport. Early in the game, Kelland shot his ball into a trap, and took quite some time getting back to the fairway.

"How many shots did you have in that trap?" teased one of his companions when he finally joined up with them again.

Kelland replied, "Four."

Another companion chuckled. "We distinctly heard eight," he said.

Kelland fairly snapped the answer. "Remember where we are," he growled. "Four of them were echoes."

An attribute many people do not possess is the ability to think quickly, although most of us wish we could.

Golfer "Lighthorse" Harry Cooper applied for a job as a professional at a country club in Hawaii. Though he'd been spoken of highly in the press, the owners of the club wanted to see what Cooper could do. So he spent several hours shooting straight and powerful balls to demonstrate his ability.

The owners, however, still looked dubious. They wanted grandstanding. So Cooper announced his greatest shot. Without explaining why, he borrowed a wristwatch from one of the owners, placed it underneath his golf ball, then hit the ball carefully.

But when Cooper went for the watch, he saw the crystal had been shattered. He hadn't expected this. Maintaining his equanimity, Cooper managed a confident smile as his mind raced ahead.

After only a split-second hesitation, Cooper gave the watch back to its owner. "The trick of that shot," he explained, as if he'd known it all along, "is to crack the crystal without damaging the watch itself."

ONE OF THE MOST BRILLIANT Supreme Court Justices was not so illustrious when it came to his favorite hobby, golf. But he was persistent at it, playing every weekend at his country club and paying the club's professional for lessons.

One day, several weeks after undertaking his series of lessons, the Justice spent twenty minutes practicing his swing without ever hitting the ball. His aim was careful, his grip sturdy, his swing powerful to say the least, but every stroke was off by several inches.

Finally, the Justice gave up in fury. But holding to the dignity of his office, he said only, "Tut! Tut!" from between clenched teeth.

The professional smiled understandingly and offered a bit of advice to the jurist. "Sir," he said, "you'll never learn to play golf with *them* words."

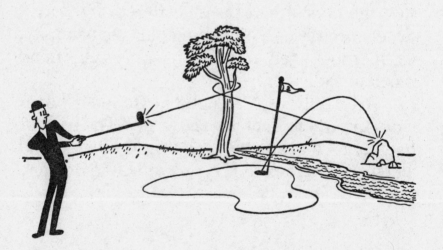

There was a young reform rabbi whose hobby was golf. Having a large congregation, however, he didn't often have time to relax. He missed playing very badly.

So the rabbi searched his calendar and found that he had only one free day—and not another for the next six months! But that day was a Saturday. Could he dare slip off after services on this one day for his favorite sport? The rabbi decided quickly, mumbled an apology to God, and on Saturday drove off to a course thirty miles away to play unrecognized.

Up in heaven, an angel looked down, and to his horror, he noticed who was on the golf course. Immediately, God was notified and asked what should be done.

God was greatly saddened. He leaned out of heaven, and with a mighty force, blew a strong gust of wind straight down onto the golf course. The rabbi was on the second hole when the heavenly breeze caught up with him, and that gust took the ball from the tee just as the rabbi swung. Up went the ball, straight down the fairway to make a miraculous hole in one. The angel was aghast.

"But why did you do that, Lord? Is that what you call a punishment?"

The Holy One smiled. "Think about it," said God. "Who can he tell?"


Two men sat next to each other on the train to Miami. Since it was a long trip, both were willing to chat.

One man, obviously wealthy, opened the conversation, "I'm looking forward to being at my vacation home again. I can't .wait to go golfing. I love golf. Do you play?"

The other man did not want to appear uncivilized, so he said, "Of course. I love to golf also. Why, every afternoon since my retirement I've played."

"Oh, then you must be pretty good!" said the rich man. "I play in the low seventies myself," he added modestly.

"Oh, so do I," said the second man. "Of course, if it gets any colder, I go right back to the hotel!"

Abe Seltzer was passing a golf course when he was struck in the head by a golf ball.

Seething, Abe picked up the ball and gestured wildly at the player running anxiously toward him. "I'll sue you in court for five hundred dollars!" Abe shouted angrily.

The golfer tried to excuse himself. "I hollered 'Fore!'" he said.

"All right!" answered Abe, "I'll take it."

Moore spotted Miller at the clubhouse bar one afternoon and rushed over excitedly. "I've heard about the tragedy you experienced last weekend. It must've been terrible!"

Miller sipped his martini and nodded, lowering his head with the unpleasant memory. "I was playing a twosome with old Mr. Crawford," he murmured solemnly, "and the poor guy dropped dead on the seventh green."

"And I heard you carried him all the way back to the clubhouse," Moore said, admiration gleaming in his eyes. "That was quite a job. Old Crawford must've weighed at least 250 pounds."

"Oh," Miller replied, sipping again, "carrying him wasn't difficult. What tired me was putting him down at every stroke, and then picking him up again."

THE HOT-TEMPERED GOLFER had spent 15 minutes in the rough unsuccessfully searching for a lost ball, and his patience was being worn to a frazzle. The caddy was no help.

Just as the linksman was about to give up the search in disgust, an elderly lady seated under a nearby tree called out to him: "Excuse me, sir, but will I be breaking the rules if I tell you where your ball is?"


TWO GOLFERS were marking time before they could tee off. "I suppose you heard," said one, "that Timothy Brown killed his wife."

"Yes, I heard something about it," responded the other, "but how? how did it happen?"

"Oh, with a golf club."

"Oh, is that so? How many strokes?"

# GREED & WEALTH

A wealthy man got up early one morning and decided to go for a walk before he left for his office. On his way back from walking through his neighborhood, he met the postman. He had a few minutes to spare, so he stopped for some conversation.

"I've been delivering mail here for ten years," said the postman, "and I don't think I've ever seen your face before. You're always out working at your business, and I understand you work late into the night and on weekends, too."

"Well, that's the only way I know to make money," said the rich man. "Why, even though I've got a million dollars now, there's so much more out there to be made! The only way to keep getting richer is to work harder. What about you? Don't you work hard at what you do?"

The postman was thoughtful. "Well, I have worked eight hours a day in all kinds of weather for the last twelve years. And I do a decent job of supporting my family, although nothing like this," the postman said, pointing to the mansion behind him.

Then he hesitated. "But I am richer than you are," the postman said.

"How can that be?" asked the millionaire.

The postman hefted the mail sack to his shoulders and started to walk on. He turned before he left and said quietly, "I have as much money as I want and you haven't."


ONE MILLIONAIRE was so penurious that he sold his mansion, his grounds, his horses, his boats, his cars, and his other properties, except one piece of land and turned all he owned into gold coins.

On the small plot of land he had left, he found a large tree and dug a hole in the ground to bury his coins. Then he returned to live in a hut he had had built. Daily he came to glimpse his wealth, digging it up to look at it, then returning it to the ground.

But a thief began to follow the miser, and after several weeks, he returned one night and stole all the gold. The next day the newly impoverished man was beside himself; he had lost everything.

Then a friend came by and tried to comfort him. "Do not grieve so much," the friend said. "Take a pile of stones and bury them in the hole. Make believe that the gold is still there. It will do you the same service, for when the gold was there you did not make the slightest use of it."

American editor and craftsman Elbert Hubbard made a profitable living from his Roycroft Shop in East Aurora, New York. Still, he never could have been described as a wealthy man. But he loved fine things, and was always seen lingering over some piece of artwork that especially pleased him.

On a visit to New York City, he went to a gallery showing the works of one of his favorite artists. He spent hours gazing at the canvases, whose price tags were astronomical.

His companion that day was a practical fellow. "Elbert," he asked, "why do you allow yourself to become so enthused over things you can never afford to own?"

The answer was quick and firm. "I would rather be able to appreciate things I cannot have," explained Hubbard, "than have things I cannot appreciate."


TWO OLD FELLOWS traveled together down the same road. One was an avaricious man; the other's character was of a jealous nature. They walked along together until they met up with an old crone.

The crone wanted to join the two in their walk, and so all three went on for a while. Then they came to a crossroads, and the crone announced she would take a different path now.

But she was a witch, she said, and would give two gifts. The man who made a wish first would get whatever he asked for; the other man's gift was to be double whatever the first man requested.

As it happened, neither man wanted to wish for any of the wonderful things of which they thought. The first was too greedy to want his companion to have double what he received; the second was too envious of the same thing happening to his companion.

Time passed, and still neither man had wished. Suddenly, the avaricious fellow became fearful the crone would leave and he would have nothing. So he grabbed his companion by the throat and threatened to strangle him if he did not wish for something.

The jealous man then said, "Very well, I will make my wish. I wish to be made blind in one eye."

A businessman had become wealthy through years of working very hard and of driving himself to exhaustion, with never any free moment for a social life. But he claimed he was happy with his money and did not really desire anything else.

One day, however, he realized that money in the bank wasn't enough. What he wanted was land! But land cost too much. He was unwilling to part with enough money to gain what he considered sufficient property.

A colleague, however, told him of a country far away that had *too much* land! There, they were willing to sell land for minimal amounts, and for your money they would give you as much land as you could walk around in a day, said the friend. The businessman decided to take a plane to the foreign country the very next day.

When he arrived in this far-off country, he found that everything his friend had said was true. The chief of the country said the man should lay down his money wherever he liked at dawn, and then walk as far as he wanted until the sun set again. All the land the man encompassed during the day he would then own.

The man was overjoyed, and being an aggressive sort, he pushed himself to go at a fast pace in order to cover a lot of ground. Many times during the day he became fatigued, but he would not allow himself to stop and rest. He pushed onward, greedy for more land.

Finally, the sun began to set, and the tribal chief and his men came out in search of the businessman. When they found him, it was just as they'd expected. The man's heart had given out from being pushed so hard. The men dug up six feet of land for him where he lay dead; then they took his money and walked away.

AL JOLSON once got into a quarrel with a young director over a particular musical arrangement. Jolson, a man who liked to have his own way, sometimes tried to flaunt his success.

"Listen, kid," he said contemptuously, "I've got a million dollars. What do you have?"

Evenly, the director remarked, "Friends."

THE LIMOUSINE PULLED UP in front of one of New York's poshest hotels and the doorman sprang forward to hold open the car door for Mrs. Henrietta de Rothsberg. Immediately, Mrs. de Rothsberg called for half a dozen bellboys.

The boys came running, and the lady dispatched them one by one with her suitcases, hatboxes, and wig stands. When she came to the last one, she announced regally, "And you, you can carry my son Steven."

The bellboy was aghast. Steven was a teenager, and no scrawny chicken. "But, madam," he complained, "surely the young man can walk."

Mrs. de Rothsberg was adamant. "Of course he can walk!" she explained. "But, thanks be to God, he'll never have to."

MANY WEALTHY MEN are known for their penurious habits. It is often said that millionaires make their money by watching every penny.

A cabbie once recognized Nathan Rothschild while driving the financier to his London home. When Rothschild alighted and paid his fare, the driver was disappointed to discover that the tip he received was quite small.

"You know, Mr. Rothschild," he said, "your daughter Julie gives me a much larger tip than that."

"That's all right for her," observed Rothschild dryly. "*She's* got a rich father."

# HOME

Mrs. Diamond had wheedled some money from her husband to have the house redecorated, and she hired an interior designer to help do the job.

"All right," said the decorator, "now how would you like it done? Modern?"

"Me, modern? No." said Mrs. Diamond.

"How's about French?" asked the decorator.

110

"*French?* Where would I come to have a French house?"

"Perhaps Italian provincial?"

"God forbid!"

"Well, madam, what period *do* you want?"

"What period? I want my friends to walk in, take one look, and drop dead! Period!"

MRS. MELTZER INVITED her new neighbor in for a cup of coffee, and to show her around the house.

"What a beautiful lamp!" admired the neighbor.

"Yes," said Mrs. Meltzer modestly, "I got it with Bleach-o detergent coupons."

"And I like that painting on the wall!" the neighbor went on.

"I got that with Bleach-o coupons, too."

"Oh, a piano! I've always wanted a piano."

"Well, as a matter of fact, I got that piano from Bleach-o coupons, too."

Then the neighbor tried one door handle that wouldn't budge. "What's in that room?" she asked full of curiosity.

"Bleach-o detergent! What else?"

A struggling farmer was burdened down with the support of a sick wife, seven children, and a mother-in-law, all in a one-room shack. Eventually, it grew too much for him, and he sought counsel from the rabbi.

"Do you have a goat?" asked the rabbi.

"Why, yes," answered the peasant.

"Take the goat into your home."

"But rabbi! There's no room as it is!"

"Just do as I say, and come back in a week."

So the farmer took the goat from the field, and brought it into the small house.

Next week, the peasant came again to the rabbi and said, "Rabbi, it's driving me wild."

"Do you have any chickens?" asked the rabbi.

"Yes, I have four—"

"Take them all into your home."

"But rabbi—"

"Just do as I tell you."

So the bewildered man took the chickens from their coop, and put them in his one-room home.

Next week, the farmer came to the rabbi and said, "Oh, rabbi! It's terrible! The goat's messing up the floor; the chickens are flying all over and messing everything up! We're going stark mad."

"Do you have a cow?" asked the rabbi.

"Yes," sighed the farmer.

"Bring the cow into the room," commanded the rabbi, "and come back next week."

The crestfallen man left in despair. That week he lived in hell. The cow mooed, the chickens cackled, and the goat bleated. The ever-present noise was awful. And the one-room had turned into a sty.

The following week, the man returned to the rabbi. He was thoroughly beaten. He poured out to the rabbi a pitiful tale of woe.

The rabbi listened patiently and then commanded, "Take all the animals out of the house, and put them back in the field. And come back tomorrow."

The man did as he was told. When he returned the following day, the rabbi asked, "Nu? How are things?"

The farmer replied, "Oh, rabbi, everything's wonderful. And so quiet! So roomy!"


Children often have a refreshing sense of the meaning of things that adults seem to have lost.

One army family of six was temporarily domiciled in a small hotel suite until a house could be made available to them on the army base. A captain came to visit the officer and his cramped family to apologize for the inconvenience.

The youngest child had an appealing manner and quickly was seated on the captain's knee. "Isn't it too bad that you don't have a home?" the captain asked the boy ruefully.

"Oh, we have a home," explained the tot carefully. "We just don't have a house to put it in."

# HORSE RACING

KENTUCKIANS are proud of their annual horserace, the Derby. It brings national notoriety and visitors from all over the country.

One hotel in Louisville used to name a room in honor of the Derby winner each year. Thus there was a Zev Room, a Gallant Fox Room, and a Whirlaway Room.

But in 1946 the hotel gave up that custom. Why? The horse that won in 1946 was named "Assault."

A HORSE PLAYER was recounting his doleful experiences at the track. "I had a very strange dream the other night. I kept dreaming about hats—all kinds of hats—men's hats, women's hats, witches' hats, big hats, little hats, hats, hats, hats. I decided the dream must be telling me something. So the next day I went to Bowie to try out my hunch. I bet on every horse that had a name that had something to do with hats. In the first race, I put 50 bucks on Fedora, and she came in first. The second race, I put 100 bucks on Straw Hat, and she beat the field by three lengths.

Seeing I was on a winning streak, I put 500 bucks on a nag called Blue Bonnet in the third race, and sure enough, she won by a nose. In the fourth race, I couldn't find any horse with a hat name but I felt like a winner so I put all my winnings plus another $250 on a horse called Foul Play, and she dragged in seventh in a field of eight."

"Too bad," said his friend. "By the way, who won that race?"

"Oh," he said, "some dodo with the crazy name of Yarmulka."

# INFIDELITY

A recently-married salesman was at the airport, about to leave on an extended business trip. At the last moment, he became conscience-stricken and returned home to his gorgeous bride.

No sooner was he back in her arms when the phone rang. He answered it.

"I'm not in the Navy," he said into the receiver. "How would I know?"

He hung up and returned to his bride. A few minutes later, the phone rang again.

"I'm not in the Navy," he repeated. "How would I know?"

Again he hung up. Curiosity got the better of his bride.

"Who is it, dear?" she asked.

"Oh, I don't know," he replied. "Some guy keeps calling and asking if the coast is clear!"

PETER RETURNED HOME early from a business trip and found his wife in the arms of his associate.

Reeling back, he exclaimed: "Max! I've *got* to. But *you*?"

GEORGE'S WIFE WAS becoming suspicious as George's hours became more and more irregular. One night his wife, determined to find out where he'd been spending his time, wired to five of George's friends: "George is not home. Is he spending the night with you?"

By the time George arrived home that night, his wife had received five telegrams all reading: "Yes."

At a bar in Paris, an American was drinking with three Frenchmen. "Tell me," he asked, "what is *sang froid*? Oh, I know that if you translate it, it means *cold blood*, but I'd like to know the connotation of that particular term."

"Well," answered one Frenchman, "let me try to explain. Suppose you have left your home—presumably on a business trip—and you come home unexpectedly. You find your wife in bed with your best friend. You do not get emotional; you do not get unduly upset. You smile at both of them, and you say, 'Pardon the intrusion.' Well, that is what I would call *sang froid*."

Another of the Frenchmen standing by broke in and said, "Well, I wouldn't exactly call that *sang froid*. I think *sang froid* is just unusual tact. Suppose in the same situation you wave hello to your friend and your wife who are in bed, and with complete imperturbability you say, 'Pardon the intrusion, sir. Don't mind me.

Please continue.' Well now, that's what I would call *sang froid.*"

"Ah!" broke in the third, "well, maybe, but as for me, I'd go a step further in my definition. If under the same circumstances you said, 'Pardon the intrusion. Please continue! and your best friend in bed *could* continue—well, that's what I would call *sang froid.*"

RETURNING HOME EARLY from a visit to a relative, Mrs. Williams found her husband in the arms of the nextdoor neighbor.

"John!" she screamed in outrage. "How could you!"

Her husband merely glanced back from the heated embrace and scowled, "Uh-oh, here comes Mrs. Blabbermouth! Now the whole neighborhood will know."

As death drew near, the rich young woman called her husband to her side and tearfully explained: "Arnold, I know that what I am about to tell you will come as a surprise, but I cannot die without this confession. I have been unfaithful to you with the chauffeur."

Her husband stared down coldly. "My dear," he said, "why do you suppose I gave you the poison?"

PETERSON CAME HOME at three in the morning and found his wife lying awake in bed.

"Where were you until three o'clock in the morning?" she screamed.

As she spoke, Peterson opened his bedroom closet and found a naked man cringing on the floor. "Who is this man?" Peterson demanded.

"Don't change the subject!" his wife replied.


IT WAS AFTER THE second world war had ended. Joe Dink was still in Japan waiting to be discharged. His wife, Irma Dink, was wild with anxiety and jealousy because she had read about the goings on between the American soldiers and the Japanese girls. Finally she could stand it no longer, and she wrote her husband. "Joe, hurry up and come back. What do those girls have anyway that the American girls don't?"

"Not a thing," wrote back Joe, "but what they have got, they've got here."


IT WAS IN A hotel at Miami Beach. There was a sudden knock on the door. The lady jumped up out of bed and said to her lover, "Quick! It's my husband. Jump out the window!"

The lover gasped, "Jump out of the window? Why, we're thirteen stories up!"

The lady said, "This is a helluva time to get superstitious!"

"I've been unfaithful to my wife," Lenny told his friend, "and my conscience can take no more. I'm going to confess to my wife tonight and beg her forgiveness."

That night Lenny told his wife about his extra-marital flings. Naturally she was hurt.

"Was it Mrs. Wilson?" she asked. "I know she cheats on her husband."

"I won't tell you," Lenny replied.

"Was it Mrs. Harris?"

"No, I won't say."

"Was it Mrs. Williamson?"

"Sorry, but I can't tell you."

"Well," retorted the angered wife, "if you won't tell me who they are, I won't forgive you."

The next day Lenny ran into his friend, who asked if his wife had forgiven him.

"No, she didn't," Lenny explained, "but she gave me three swell leads."

Accurate diction was not the only passion of Noah Webster, America's great lexicographer. One day, Mrs. Webster entered the parlor to discover her husband locked in embrace with their maidservant.

"Noah!" she spluttered, "I *am* surprised!"

Mr. Webster disentangled himself and immediately regained his professional composure. "No, my dear," he replied. "It is *I* who am surprised. You are merely astonished."

WALLACE DASHED WILDLY into his apartment and found his wife in the kitchen. "Alice!" he gasped. "We've gotta move out of here right away. I just found out that the superintendent in this building makes love to every woman in it but one."

"Yeah, I know," his wife replied calmly. "That's that stuck up thing on the fifth floor."

Sinclair had been married for ten years and had lived nine of them in agony. He was unbelievably jealous of his coquettish wife. For years, he had suspected she was having an affair with his business partner. Finally, he could stand the tension no longer, and hired a detective to trail her.

A few days later, the detective reported to Sinclair.

"Well, did you follow them?"

"Oh, yes," said the detective, "I have the report here. Last night, she left your home about 8:30, and then she met a man on the corner of Reid Street and Montgomery Place. They strolled around for about 15 minutes. Then they got into a car, and went down to Patmore Lane. There they parked for a half hour, and he made advances to her, to which she ungrudgingly responded. Then they drove to the Franconia Hotel. I checked at the desk, and found out that they were occupying Room 311. Fortunately, Room 311 faced the street. So I climbed a tree opposite their window, peered in, and saw them both standing there completely nude, fondling each other."

"And then?" cried Mr. Sinclair. "What happened then?"

"Oh, well, then they pulled down the shade!"

"Oh!" moaned Sinclair, "What a tragedy! Always to doubt! Never to know!"


To start a small Christmas Club for his wife, Miller agreed to give her fifty cents every time she favored him. Mrs. Miller always dropped the coins into a small piggy bank she kept in her closet.

At Christmas the bank was opened, and Miller was shocked to see a number of one, five, and ten dollar bills among the contents.

"Wait a minute," he told his wife, "I only

gave you fifty cents each time. Where did these bills come from?"

"Well," his wife replied, "do you think everybody is as cheap as you?"

A jealous wife was searching her husband's pockets when she came across a card on which was scribbled, "Peggy Brown, Center 722." She confronted him with the card.

"Oh, that's nothing," her husband explained. "Peggy Brown is just the name of a race horse I bet on."

"Oh, yeah? Well then, what does this 'Center' mean?" she demanded.

"That's the name of the street where my bookmaker lives," he countered quickly.

"How about 722?" she challenged. "Get out of that one if you can!"

"Why, dear, those are the odds—seven to two!" he said in hurt surprise.

His wife was forced to give up her interrogation.

But the following night when he came home he found his wife standing in the doorway.

"Anything new today, honey?" he asked.

"Oh, nothing much," she sneered, "except that your horse called up!"

The salesman walked into the hotel and noticed a pretty blonde lounging in a big easy chair.

He threw her a warm look which she returned with a smile and a nod. In a minute they walked over to the register arm in arm. The salesman signed, "Mr. and Mrs. Mark J. Hamilton."

The next morning the salesman checked

out. When he went to the cashier, he got a bill for $173. "What!" he shouted at the cashier, "I have only been here one night!"

"I know," said the cashier, "but your wife has been here for two months."

A HUSBAND COMPLAINED that his wife was a liar. "What makes you say that?" said his friend.

"Well," said the husband, "She came home this morning and told me she spent the night with Eleanor."

"Well," replied the friend, "Maybe she did. How do you know she's lying?"

"How do I know, because *I* spent the night with Eleanor."

# INSULT

GROUCHO MARX had a rejoinder for every straight line. Once, the behavior of a noted Hollywood star was the topic of conversation between Groucho and Arthur Murray. Sympathetically, Murray offered, "She's her own worst enemy."

Raising his eyebrows, Groucho made ready to clamp his teeth around a cigar, and then growled, "Not while I'm alive, she isn't!"


DOROTHY PARKER always had the right words to quash the insufferably superior.

A comedian once entertained at a party to which Miss Parker had been invited. The man seated next to her, full of scorn, cast a withering look at the laughing guests.

"I'm afraid I can't join in the merriment," he drawled. "I can't bear fools."

"That's strange," Miss Parker chuckled. "Your mother could."


A dapper young gentleman was going down in an elevator with five strange women. When they reached the first floor, the man stepped aside to allow them to exit first. As the last woman left the elevator, she turned and sneered, "When Women's Lib has its day, *you'll* get off first!"

"My dear lady," the gentleman replied, "I'd like to see all women free."

"You would?" the woman exclaimed, utterly surprised.

"Yes," the gentleman smiled, "I hate it when they charge."

Dorothy Parker and a friend were once discussing a celebrity whose garrulousness was unrivaled.

"She's so outspoken," observed the friend.

"By whom?" inquired Miss Parker.

AN UNBEARABLY IRRITATING MAN belonged to the same club as humorist Oliver Herford.

While conversing amiably with some companions one day, Herford saw the obnoxious fellow approach and girded himself for what might come.

"Can you imagine?" snapped the arrival. "As I passed that group of people over there, I overheard someone say that he would give me fifty dollars to leave the club!"

Herford leaned forward as if to reassure

him. "That's ridiculous!" he said. "By all means, hold out for a hundred! You'll surely get it!"

John Randolph was a well-spoken Congressman, known as an impressive debater until he was outshone by the "Great Compromiser," Henry Clay. The bitterness between Randolph and Clay was never appeased.

One day, after avoiding each other for several months, the two men found themselves walking toward each other on the same street. Seeing that neither could pass by on the narrow walk, Randolph said stubbornly, "I never give way to scoundrels."

Clay saw his way out. He stepped off the curb to pass and said, "I *always* do."

GROUCHO MARX and a friend once were strolling through a park when they passed an extremely plump and wrinkled lady walking with her husband.

"Oh, I just love nature!" the woman was cooing.

"That's loyalty," Groucho told his companion, "after what nature did to her!"

CHARLES TALLEYRAND was an adroit French

diplomat at the turn of the nineteenth century, who was known for his acid comments.

One of his rivals was Madame de Stael, a writer, intellectual, and wit in her own right. "There's a new book out," remarked Madame de Stael to Talleyrand one day, "in which the author has represented each of us in thin disguise."

"Is that so?" replied the diplomat.

"Yes. He can scarcely value your masculinity, however, for he saw fit to portray each of us as an attractive woman."

"Indeed?" said Talleyrand with equanimity. "And wrong in each case."

# INSURANCE

IT WAS BERNIE's first day as a health-insurance salesman. For his first prospect, he was given the name of the president of a big corporation. If the man bought a policy, Bernie was empowered to speed up proceedings by bringing back a urine sample for processing the same day.

Bernie was gone all morning. When he came back that afternoon, he was carrying the signed policy and a large bucket.

Pleased with himself, Bernie showed his boss the policy. "That's great," the boss smiled. "But what's in the bucket?"

"What do you mean 'what's in the bucket'?" Bernie puffed with pride, "I sold the company a group policy!"


Moishe slipped in front of a department store. In the freak accident, he broke both his legs. After several months, all the bones healed. His family now persuaded him to sue the store for damages on the grounds that he'd been permanently crippled.

So Moishe got himself a wheelchair and a

lawyer and he sued. And despite testimony from the insurance company's doctors, Moishe's pitiable appearance won him the sympathy of the court. He was awarded $30,000.

When the insurance man came to deliver the check, he was shaking with fury. "We know you aren't permanently crippled," he stated. "And, so help me, we're going to follow you all the days of your life until you stand up and walk out of that wheelchair. And when you do, we'll take your picture and sue you for all this money and more!"

But Moishe maintained he was permanently crippled. The man handed him the check, and then begrudgingly asked what Moishe would do with it.

"Well, me and my wife, we've always wanted to travel," said Moishe. "So we're going to fly to Scandinavia, and then on through Switzerland, Italy, Greece—and I don't care what agents and spies with cameras are following me because I'm going in my wheelchair. And then, of course, we'll go to Israel; then to Persia and India, and across to Japan and the Philippines—and I'm still going to be in this wheelchair. So I don't care about your people who are following. And from there we are going all across Australia, and then to South America, and then all the way up to Mexico and through the western U.S.A. and cross-country to Canada and across again to France."

He paused for breath, and then went on. "And there, we're going to visit a place called Lourdes. And there, you're going to see a miracle!"

To INCREASE CIRCULATION, a certain newspaper advertised an accident policy free to all new subscribers. A few days later, this advertisement appeared in the paper:

"P. J. Melton subscribed to our paper and was given a free accident policy. On his way home from work, he fell down a flight of stairs and broke an arm, a jaw, and both legs. The accident policy paid him $1,000. *You may be the lucky one tomorrow.*"

# JAIL

Frederick II of Prussia, also known as Frederick the Great, instituted social reforms and improvements throughout his country. One day, he unexpectedly visited a prison to inspect the facilities. The head jailer was dismayed to be asked to show the King through the jail itself to see the conditions personally.

As Frederick proceeded through the jail, the convicted men came running up to him, pleading innocence and begging for pardons. The King listened to all, and walked on. He became surrounded by men claiming they were not guilty.

One man, however, stayed in his corner. The King was surprised. "You, there," he called. "Why are you here?"

"Robbery, Your Majesty," stated the prisoner.

"And are you guilty?" asked Frederick.

"Entirely guilty, Your Majesty. I richly deserve my punishment."

The King parted the throng with his walking stick and pointed it at the jailer. "Warden," he said, "release this guilty wretch at once. I will not have him here in jail where by example he will corrupt all the splendid innocent people who occupy it."


A FEISTY, overage delinquent once faced Judge Kenesaw Mountain Landis and tried to talk his way out of a five-year sentence for his misdeeds.

"But, Your Honor, I'll be dead long before that," complained the old man. "I'm a very sick man—I can't possibly do five years!"

"Well," the judge said firmly, "you can try, can't you?"


The local Ladies' Auxiliary was writing letters to convicts in the state prison to make their lives a little brighter. But the young bride of one attorney was having a particularly difficult time getting started. What should she call him? She only knew his number.

Finally, she decided on the casual approach: "Dear 47928693. Or may I call you 479?"


A prisoner in an ancient kingdom was once judged guilty of a crime by his king and sentenced to death. The prisoner begged the king for a reprieve. If his execution were delayed for one year, the prisoner promised to teach the king's horse to fly.

Surprised, but too curious not to give it a try, the king agreed, and the prisoner went home. A neighbor came by to congratulate him, but also asked, "Why delay the inevitable?"

The condemned man explained, "It's not inevitable. The odds are four-to-one in my favor: (1) The king might die. (2) I might die. (3) The horse might die. (4) I might teach the horse to fly."

The governor was inspecting a new state psychiatric hospital. While being shown through the isolation wards, he was struck by a man of distinguished appearance sitting on a bunk reading a copy of the *New York Times*, and wearing nothing but a fancy silk top hat.

The inmate rose immediately, bowed to his guests, and said to the governor, "Sir, you must be curious as to why I sit here in the nude."

"Well, yes," the governor replied.

"It is not mysterious at all," said the inmate. "Since this cell is air-conditioned, and I enjoy complete privacy, clothing is not necessary for warmth, modesty, or adornment. So why should I bother with it at all?"

"That's all very true," the governor agreed, taken aback by the inmate's rationality. "But in that case, why the top hat?"

The inmate shrugged. "Oh, well! Someone might come."

# LABOR

Technology has been viewed as a creeping
menace, but inventor Thomas Edison saw it as a
useful aspect of progress.

One day, after Edison had lunched with a
friend, the two men passed by a construction site
and paused to watch a giant machine moving a
mound of earth.

"That machine will put a great number of
men out of work!" decried Edison's luncheon
companion.

The great inventor paused, then said sar-
castically, "And think how many more men
could be put to work if they would move that
earth with teaspoons!"

Direct confrontation is often the least effective way of handling hostilities. Accordingly, the president of one factory tried a unique approach when faced with a crippling strike of assembly-line workers.

"All right, boys," he said soothingly. "As long as you're going to be here overnight, you may as well be comfortable." Whereupon he ordered blankets and pillows—and brandy—for all. Then he went home.

A little later in the evening, he called his plant representative to see how it was going. When he'd ascertained that the brandy was nearly gone and the men were feeling fine, the president sent for a group of ladies to entertain his workers.

Some more time elapsed. Then the president made his final move. He invited the wives of the strikers to join their husband at their vigil.

Within minutes, there wasn't a man left in the plant.


WHEN THE NOONTIME WHISTLE blew at the construction site, O'Toole limped out for lunch.

"Why the limp?" his foreman asked. "You got a sore foot?"

"There's a nail in my shoe," O'Toole moaned.

"Then why don't you take it out?"

"What?" O'Toole replied indignantly. "On my lunch hour!"

A factory in the Northwest operated on a single, huge electrical generator, and the plant fell into complete helplessness on the day the power source broke down. Repairmen tried everything possible, but without success. Finally, since inactivity was an extravagance the factory could not afford, the president sent to the parent company for an expert.

When the man arrived, everyone at the plant crowded around him. The president directed him to the generating room and said, "Jones, I hope you can help us." The man said nothing, but began to slowly examine every pipe, every dial, every switch on the generator.

Finally, Jones stopped in front of a particular pipe and produced a small hammer from his tool kit. His audience watched in awe. Gingerly, he felt with his fingers for the right spot. Then he tapped the hammer carefully at just the right angle. Immediately, the generator began to run again.

The president smiled in relief and said, "Well done, sir! And what is your fee?"

"Five hundred and five dollars," said Jones.

The president was suddenly prudent. "Five hundred and five dollars for simply hitting the pipe with a hammer?"

"Ah," explained Jones. "For that, five dollars. For knowing *where* to hit, five hundred dollars."

TWO LABORERS STOPPED in front of a jewelry store window to admire a tray of sparkling diamonds. "How would you like to have your pick?" asked one.

"I'd rather have my shovel," replied the other. "I could get more that way."

GREENSTEIN AND HIS FAMILY decided to move from New York to the Pacific Northwest.

"But what will you do there?" asked his friends.

"I'm strong," said Greenstein. "I'll be a lumberjack."

So the family moved West. Greenstein went out to look for a job as a lumberjack. The first foremen he met was impressed with his muscles, but wanted a physical demonstration of strength. He pointed to a tree with a twelve-inch trunk and asked Greenstein to cut it down. Greenstein did it in one minute.

"I can't believe it," said the astonished foreman. "My best cutter couldn't do that tree in less than four minutes! Please, Mr. Greenstein, do just one more so I know my eyes aren't deceiving me."

He pointed to a tree 16 inches thick. Greenstein downed it in two minutes.

"That's unbelievable, Mr. Greenstein. That tree would have taken any of my men ten minutes! Tell me, where did you work before this?"

"Well," said Greenstein modestly, "when I learned lumberjacking, I was in the Sahara."

"In the Sahara?" The foreman was incredulous. "But there are no trees in the Sahara!"

"Not any more there aren't."


A woman was showing a contractor through the second floor of her new house, advising him what colors to paint the rooms. "I'd like the bedroom done in blue," she instructed.

The contractor walked over to the window and shouted: "Green side up! Green side up!"

"I want the bathroom in white!" continued the woman.

Again the contractor yelled out the window, "Green side up! Green side up!"

"The halls should be done in gray!"

Again the contractor shouted out the window, "Green side up! Green side up!"

"Every time I give you a color, you shout 'Green side up!" the woman snapped angrily.

"I'm sorry, ma'am." the contractor explained. "But I've got three dumb laborers down there below putting in the lawn."

Jake, a plumber, died. His union called a meeting to raise money for his bereft, poverty-stricken wife and children. Contributions were to be voluntary.

One of the union members got up and made such a stirring speech that half the men started to weep and sob out loud. There wasn't a dry eye in the congregation.

But one man sat there unmoved, with not a

trace of emotion showing on his face. His neighbor turned to him and said, "How come you're not crying?" "I'm not a member here," was the answer.

SOME PEOPLE deal with their problems head on; other individuals take an easier approach.

In the 1930s, General Somervell was administering the WPA and was confronted with a "sit-down" strike. Union members took over space in a public building and would not leave.

The police had tried before without much success. This time Somervell simply locked all the building's bathrooms, and left with the keys. The strike was over in six hours.

# LAWYERS & THE COURT

QUICK-WITTED trial lawyer A. S. Trude once found his next-door neighbor, Dr. Frank Billings, serving as medical expert in a case against his client.

Casting about for a way to handle the physician's testimony to his own client's benefit, Trude began his cross-examination by asking the doctor, "Was Marshall Field one of your patients?"

The doctor answered that he was.

"Where is Mr. Field now?" Trude inquired. Though Field had died of natural causes, Dr. Billings still had to answer, "Dead."

Trude then asked about patients named Pullman, Cudahy, and Armour.

All of these wealthy men had died naturally. Yet when asked where these patients were now, the doctor, in each case, was compelled to reply that the man was dead.

Trude then turned from the witness stand and walked back toward his client. "That's all," he said to Dr. Billings. "Thank you."

He won the case.

A peddler was brought to court by a cop who found him peddling without a license. While the peddler was sitting in the courtroom waiting his turn to appear before the bench, he listened to the proceedings of other cases.

A prostitute was brought up before the judge. The judge asked her, "What do you have to say?"

"Oh," she said, "I was minding my own business. I was standing in front of an attractive store window just looking at some shoes. Along came this cop, and said I was hustling."

"Well, were you?" said the judge.

"No, not at all. I'm absolutely innocent."

"Naturally," said the judge. "Your record proves that! You've been before this court six times this year. I fine you $100 and 30 days in the cooler."

The next woman, brought up on the same charge, again offered a lame excuse; and the judge, in a fury, fined her $250, with two months in jail.

The third girl arraigned said, "Your Honor, I was caught redhanded. I was soliciting. I have nothing more to say."

"Well," said the judge, "at least you're honest about it. I'll let you off with a $25 fine, and don't let it happen again."

Then the peddler was brought before the bench. "How do you plead?" asked the judge.

"Your Honor, what shall I tell you? You're a

wise judge; you see through everything. Your
honor, I'm guilty. I'm a whore!"

Late Chief Justice of the Supreme Court Charles
Evans Hughes enjoyed the humor of one of the
more modest Supreme Court Justices, Benjamin
Cardozo. One occasion the Chief Justice
recalled was a boat outing the Justices had
planned in order to relieve some of their recent
strains.

The dedicated Justice Cardozo, a man
totally dispassionate in the courtroom, was
losing an all-too-human battle with the steady
rolling of the boat. Sympathetically, Chief
Justice Hughes put his hand on his associate's
back and said, "Can I do anything for you?"

"Yes," replied Cardozo, "overrule the motion."

ONE HIGH-RANKING JUDGE tells of the time that he arrived late to a funeral. The first man he saw was Hugo Black, controversial Supreme Court Judge. Black was only present because he was expected to be; in fact, he'd always felt a dislike for the dead man.

The tardy guest tiptoed over to Black and asked him, "How far has the service gone?"

Black muttered to the other judge, "They just opened the defense."

During the days of the great gold rush, many new towns were born in the West. Rough men populated these towns, and justice, in the form of the sheriff or a judge, could often be bought and sold for an inflated price.

In one small town in northern California, gold veined the nearby hills, making competition keen for the fortune to be found there. It is not surprising that many rival mining claims ended up in court.

On the morning of the trial of one of these claims, the judge made this unusual announcement:

"Gentlemen, this court has in hand a check from the plaintiff in this case for ten thousand dollars and a check for the defendant for fifteen thousand dollars. The court will return five thousand dollars to the defendant. Then we will try the case strictly on its merits."

One of our more famous senior senators spent many years as a trial lawyer before running for public office. He says the most important thing he learned in the courtroom is the value of a brief speech.

He tells of the time he was opposed by a long-winded prosecutor who spent over four hours summing up the case for the jury on the hottest day in July.

When time came for the future senator to sum up, he approached the judge quietly. The hum of the fans was the only sound in the courtroom other than that of the jurors taking out their handkerchiefs to mop their brows and stifle their yawns.

"Your Honor," said the lawyer, "I will follow the example of my friend who has just concluded, and will submit the case without argument."

He won the case.


Clarence Darrow's way with words was not restricted only to the courtroom.

A worried litigant found her troubles were over the minute she retained Darrow; the lawyer defended her brilliantly and won her case hands down.

When it was all over, the client said to him, "Oh, Mr. Darrow, how can I ever show my appreciation?"

"My dear woman," Darrow responded with equanimity, "ever since the Phoenicians invented money, there has been only one answer to that question."

A lawyer had scheduled a business trip to New York, and a colleague had suggested he call on Miss Agatha Jane Foote while in town. "It'll be an unforgettable experience," the colleague promised. "She's no ordinary trollope, I assure you."

The first night of his New York stay, the lawyer took a cab and got out in front of one of the finest brownstones on Fifth Avenue. He rang the bell, and a maid ushered him in. After presenting his card, he was led into an elegantly furnished drawing room and invited to make himself comfortable. Miss Foote would be down shortly.

While waiting, the lawyer stepped over to a huge floor-to-ceiling bookcase and examined the gilt-bound works. Among the many tomes was a 20-volume set of Corpus Jurus.

A few moments later, Miss Foote stepped down the curved staircase in a most elegant evening gown. The lawyer stood stunned. She was indeed gorgeous!

But he was further stunned to find Miss Foote's conversation urbane, charming, and witty. He turned to the bookcase and remarked, "Miss Foote, I notice a set of Corpus Jurus on your shelves. Did you ever study law?"

"Yes," she replied, "I'm a graduate of the Columbia Law School."

"Is that so?" the lawyer continued. "Then how did you ever get into this business?"

"Oh!" Miss Foote shrugged, "I must have been very lucky."

AT A MURDER TRIAL, the jury had been debating for sixteen hours. Wearily the jury members returned to the jury box. Just before the verdict was disclosed, the foreman turned to the judge and said, "Your honor, may we ask a question?"

The judge said, "Of course, speak up."

"Well," said the foreman, "Before we pass judgment, we'd like to know if the defendant prefers AC or DC current?"

The witness was being interrogated rudely by the attorney for the plaintiff.

"What did you say your business was?" the lawyer asked.

"I'm a day laborer," came the reply.

"A day laborer, eh?" snarled the lawyer. "What would you consider your social status is in this world as a day laborer?"

"I don't think it's very high," the witness shrugged, but I feel I'm doing better than my father before me."

"What was your father?"

"He was a *shyster lawyer*," came the witness' retort.


Mr. Levy went to see his lawyer. He was quite distraught. "What am I going to do?" he asked. "Finkel is suing me for breaking an irreplaceable jar of his!"

The lawyer seemed calm. "Don't worry, Mr. Levy," he soothed. "We have at least three lines of defense. In the first place, we will prove that you never borrowed the jar from Finkel. In the second place, we'll prove that when you borrowed the jar, it was already damaged beyond repair. And in the third place, we'll prove that when you returned it, it was in absolutely perfect condition."

# MARITAL LIFE

"My wife," said Koblinsky, "is so educated, so well read, that she can talk for hours and hours on any subject you name."

"Huh," scoffed Michaelson, "that's nothing. My wife can talk for hours and hours and doesn't even require a subject."

LENNY AND MILDRED had been having marital difficulties, so they repaired to a marriage counselor. At the session, Lenny complained that Mildred didn't prepare proper meals for him. Mildred's complaint was that Lenny hadn't been fulfilling his conjugal obligations. After much altercation, the marriage counselor straightened things out; the final verdict was that Milly was to go to cooking school, and Lenny was to sleep with Milly semi-annually.

Going down the stairs, from the office, Milly, was glowing with satisfaction. As they reached the street, however, a troubling thought struck her. She took Lenny by the hand, looked up into his eyes, and said: "Tell me, Lenny, how many times a week is semi-annually?"

153

Often the only one able to get the better of a wit is his wife. Mrs. George Bernard Shaw listened one day to her husband's clever logic promoting men as wiser than women.

"Of course, you're right, my dear," responded Mrs. Shaw placidly. "After all, you married me and I you."

IT WAS A FEARFUL NIGHT. Lightning shot through the sky and the thunder roared in blasts that would frighten anybody. The rain came down in sheets.

The door of a little bakery opened and a drenched man came up to the counter and said, "Let me have two bagels."

The baker looked at him incredulously. "What," said the baker, "you came out on a night like this just for two bagels? That's all?"

"Yes, that's all," answered the man. "That's all I need. Just one for me and one for Pauline."

"Who's Pauline?" asked the baker.

"Oh what the hell difference is it to you?" answered the man. "Pauline is my wife. Who do you think she is? Would my mother send me out on a night like this?"

PORTER PACED BACK and forth in the doctor's waiting room while his wife underwent a complete physical examination inside. Finally the doctor opened the door and summoned the husband. "To be blunt, Mr. Porter," he said gravely, "I don't like the looks of your wife."

"Neither do I," Porter responded, "but she's great with the kids."

AFTER A TWO-YEAR absence, Chuck returned to his wife with hat in hand and tried to explain what he had been doing during his absence.

"I've been a lion tamer, honey. I'd go into a cage, snap my whip, and next thing you knew I had that lion eating out of my hand."

"You ain't no lion *tamer*," his wife snapped back. "You're a lyin' *bastard*."

THE NEW NEIGHBOR joined the mah johngg group for the first time, and all the ladies gaped at the huge diamond she wore.

"It's the third most famous diamond in the world," she told the women confidentially. "First is the Hope diamond, then the Kohinoor diamond, and then this one—the Rabinowitz diamond."

"It's beautiful!" admired one woman enviously. "You're so lucky!"

"Not so lucky," the newcomer maintained. "Unfortunately, with the famous Rabinowitz diamond, I have received the famous Rabinowitz curse."

"And what is that?" wondered the women.

The woman heaved an enormous sigh. "Mr. Rabinowitz," she said.


THE HUSBAND CAME HOME drunk again. His wife couldn't stand it. She screamed at him, "If you don't stop this damnable drinking, I'm going to kill myself."

The hapless husband retorted, "Promises, that's all I get. Promises."


TWO WOMEN MET again after many years and began exchanging histories. "Whatever happened to your son?" asked one woman.

"Oh, what a tragedy!" moaned the other. "My son married a no-good who doesn't lift a finger around the house. She can't cook, she can't sew a button on a shirt, all she does is sleep.

My poor boy brings her breakfast in bed, and all day long she stays there, loafing, reading, eating candy!"

"That's terrible," sympathized the first woman. "And what about your daughter?"

"Oh, she's got a good life. She married a man who's a living doll! He won't let her set foot in the kitchen. He gives her breakfast in bed, and makes her stay there all day, resting, reading, and eating chocolates."


A BATTLING COUPLE had had the worst spat of their marriage. Enraged and disgusted, the husband grabbed his coat and stormed out of the house.

To cool his ire, the sizzling spouse took the subway to Grand Central and visited some of the local bars to try to forget his troubles. Before long he was beginning to feel his oats.

By 2 A.M., the hapless husband decided that he was soused enough to take anything his wife could mete out. He left a bar and started walking up Eighth Avenue, looking for the subway station.

As he neared Madison Square Garden, he looked up and there in bright neon lights glared the sign: *Big Fight Tonight.* He paused, refocussed his eyes, and sighed:

"Ah, home at last!"

Max had been living with his shrewish wife for thirty years. But he couldn't stand the nagging any longer. He consulted his friend Shmuel about what to do.

"Why not do her in?" suggested Shmuel.

"If I do that I'll be thrown in jail. I don't want to spend the rest of my life in prison."

Shmuel considered, then he said, "Well, why don't you buy her a car? She can't drive. Maybe she'll have an accident, and her death won't be on your head."

So Max bought his wife a little sportscar. But when he met Shmuel a week later, he still looked sad. "She drives it perfectly," said Max. "I threw my money away."

Shmuel knew what was wrong. "That car you bought her was too small. Why don't you get her a large car that will be hard to handle? She's bound to get into an accident with a big sedan."

So Max bought his wife a huge Cadillac. But that didn't work either. "She drives that one perfectly, too," he told Shmuel a week later. "What do I do now?"

"Well, there's one other thing you can try. Splurge and get her a Jaguar."

So Max bought his wife a Jaguar. A week later, he was all smiles.

"So what happened?" Shmuel asked him.

"Wonderful!" exclaimed Max. "One bite, and she was finished!"

MR. GOLD HAD BEEN married for many years when he had to go to Paris for a business trip. In that city of love, he easily fell victim to the amorous advances of the pretty mademoiselles.

But somehow Mrs. Gold found out about it. She wired her husband at his hotel: "COME HOME! WHY SPEND MONEY THERE FOR WHAT YOU CAN GET HERE FOR FREE?"

The next day, she received a cable in reply: "I KNOW YOU AND YOUR BARGAINS!"

Mrs. Meyerowitz met Mrs. Goldstein for a cup of tea one afternoon.

"Did you hear that the Martinsons' stove exploded last night?" began Mrs. Meyerowitz. "Mr. and Mrs. Martinson were blown right out the front door and into the street!"

"If that's true," quipped Mrs. Goldstein, "that's the first time they've gone out together in thirty years."

EVERYONE ACKNOWLEDGED that the Jacobys were the happiest family in the neighborhood. They never quarreled about anything and always seemed to get along. One day, at a cocktail party, the neighbors and friends gathered around Jacoby and asked him how he could account for the marvelous success of his marriage.

"Oh," he said proudly, "Sadie and I made an agreement when we got married. She would make all the small decisions and I would make all the big decisions. And we've kept to that policy through all the years of our marriage."

"Like what kind of big and small decisions?" asked the curious audience.

"Well," explained Jacoby, "she makes the small decisions like who my son Milton is going to marry; who my daughter Jeanette should go out with; where we should go on our summer vacation; and how much we should spend, for example, on a bar mitzvah present for Tom Seltzer's son; how much we should pay for the maid. That kind of thing, you know."

"And the big decisions?" pursued the crowd.

"Oh," said Jacoby modestly, "I make the fundamental decisions. I decide whether the United States should resume relations with China. I decide how much money Congress should approve for Israel. And I decide who would be the best candidate for president."

POOR MRS. EISENBERG was beside herself. Her husband had left her, and her daughter Sally was thirty-two years old and still unmarried. She thought about it and worried about it and finally decided to take some action.

"Sally," she said, "I think you ought to put an advertisement in the paper." Sally was aghast at the thought.

"No, listen," said Mrs. Eisenberg, "it sounds wild, but I think we should try it. You don't put your name in, just a box number. Here, I wrote one up already." And she showed Sally an ad she had devised:

*Charming Jewish Girl, Well-Educated, Fine Cook, Would like to Meet Kind, Intelligent, Educated, Jewish Gentleman. Object: Matrimony.*

Sally was embarrassed, but she couldn't talk her mother out of it. So into the paper the ad went. And Sally went every day to see if there were any replies.

A few days later, there was a letter for her. Sally ran home to her mother flushed with excitement. "Look!" she cried.

"Well, hurry up and open it!" urged Mrs. Eisenberg. So Sally tore open the envelope and unfolded the letter. Then she began to cry.

"What's the matter?" asked Mrs. Eisenberg.

Sally's sobs got even louder. "It's from papa!"

Mr. and Mrs. Mandelbaum decided the only solution to their marital problems was in divorce. So they went to see the rabbi.

The rabbi was concerned about the three children and was reluctant to see the family broken up. He thought that if he could stall the couple maybe they would work it out together.

"Well," said the rabbi, "there's no way of dividing three children. What you'll have to do is live together one more year. You'll have a fourth child, and then, it will be easy to arrange a proper divorce. You'll take two children, and he'll take two."

"Nothing doing," said Mrs. Mandelbaum. "Rabbi, if I depended on him, I wouldn't even have had these three!"


Benny had worked as a tailor for many years. Came the time when he wished to retire, but his savings account was spare.

"Miriam," he confided to his wife, "I'm tired. I want to retire, but I don't know how we're going to afford it."

"Don't worry," said Miriam, "I have plenty of money." And she produced a bankbook with regular deposits stretching back the entire forty years of their marriage.

"Where did this come from?" cried Benny in amazement.

"Well," said Miriam softly, "every time,

during the last forty years, that we made love, I put five dollars away."

Benny threw his arms around his wife, and impulsively cried out, "Oh Miriam! For heaven's sake, you should have told me. If I had only known, I would have given you all my business."

Golda and Becky got together for their usual morning cup of coffee.

"Did you meet that new woman who moved in across the street?" asked Golda.

"Did I ever!" exclaimed Becky. "She couldn't stop complaining about her husband."

"Believe me, there's nothing worse than a complaining wife," said Golda. "Now take me; my husband drinks too much, he gambles, he stays out late—a worse husband you never saw in your life. But do *I* ever say anything to anybody?"

In the midst of a heated argument, Mrs. Cratchit lost her patience and began beating her diminutive husband.

In terror he ran into the bedroom and crawled under the bed, his wife in hot pursuit.

"Come out!" she cried.

"No!" Cratchit shouted back from under the bed. "I'll show you who's boss in this house!"

HYDE'S WIFE WAS a constant nag, forever comparing her husband to his more affluent friends. "The Marshalls have a new car and the Murrays just bought a new house," she complained. "All our friends live ten times better than we do. If we don't move into a more expensive apartment they'll all be laughing at us!"

One night her beleaguered husband came home and told her, "Well, we'll soon be living in a more expensive apartment. The landlord just doubled our rent."

A COLLEGE FRESHMAN wrote his father to announce that he'd landed a part in the school play. "I play a man who's been married for 25 years," the student wrote.

"Congratulations, son," his father wrote back. "Keep up the good work and next year maybe they'll give you a speaking part."

"BUT DARLING," the henpecked husband protested, "I'm doing everything I can to make you happy!"

"You don't do one thing my first husband did to make me happy!" she pouted.

"And what's that ?" the harassed husband asked.

"He died!"

THE HONEYMOON WAS barely over when the young couple got into their first argument. The subject was money.

"Before we were married," the wife cried "you told me you were well off."

"I was," he growled. "But I didn't know it."

YONKEL AND FLORRIE were invited to a dinner party at Yonkel's boss's home on Long Island. Yonkel knew he had to go, but he was afraid the people there would be much smarter than he. So he instructed Florrie to keep her mouth shut and not to say anything if she could help it. If someone asked her a direct question, she was to answer with just a yes or a no.

Florrie agreed, and the two set off nervously for the party. Yonkel said hardly a word the whole evening, and Florrie said nothing at all. But this state of affairs began to upset the hostess, who thought that it was her job to draw her guests into the conversation.

So the boss's wife turned to Florrie and said to her kindly, "Tell me, are you acquainted with Beethoven?"

Florrie had been silent for so long, she became flustered at being addressed directly. She stammered and fell all over herself and finally said, "Oh, yes, I met him just the other day on the A train to Coney Island."

The hostess and all the guests were mortified; it took them a few minutes to regain their composure. But eventually, the hostess found her tongue again and smoothed things over by chattering with her other guests.

After all the good-byes were said and Florrie was in the car with Yonkel, the husband lashed out at her. "I thought I told you to keep quiet!" he shouted. "You embarrassed me beyond belief, I hope you know that."

Florrie was crestfallen. Yonkel continued. "My God," he ranted, "There wasn't a single person there who didn't know that the A train does not go to Coney Island!"

The Marriage Counselor was advising the bride to be. "The first thing I must tell you is that if you want to retain the interest of your husband you must never completely disrobe in front of him when retiring. Always keep a little mystery about you."

About two months later, the husband said to his bride, "Tell me, Jane, is there any insanity in your family?"

"Of course not," she responded hotly. "Why do you ask such a question?"

"Well," said he, "I was merely wondering why, during the last two months since we're married, when you go to bed you never take off your hat."

Even a worm will turn, and the timid little husband confronted his wife and bellowed, "When are we eating?"

"Eight o'clock," she answered in a matter of fact way.

"Eight o'clock!" he roared, "When I come home at six o'clock from work! Tonight, we eat at seven o'clock, that's my deadline! And what's more," he continued, "don't give me any more canned salmon."

She turned, slightly astonished. The shy one, no longer shy, continued, "And set out my best suit—because I have got a date tonight with the blonde stenographer from the office. I'm sick and tired of this humdrum life, and I'm going out dancing."

The lady couldn't believe her ears. Carried

away with his newly-found power, the husband continued, "And put out my little black tie! And when I'm all dressed and ready to go—" he said glaring at her full in the face, "do you know who's going to tie it on me?"

The big woman rose to her full height. "Yes," she said, "I certainly do! The man from the Jamestown Funeral Parlor."

ONE NIGHT WHILE RETURNING HOME from work, the henpecked husband stopped off for a few stiff shots to prepare himself for another night of tongue-lashing. One drink led to another, and by the time he left the bar, he was properly stewed. Passing the zoo, he decided on a short nap. He opened a small door, crawled into the lion's cage, and fell asleep with his head on the lion's mouth.

The next morning his wife searched wildly across town for him, and finally located him, still sleeping in the lion's cage. Shaking her fist at the little man, she shouted: "Come on out of there, you coward!"


Sometimes it's difficult to see what attracts people to their mates. One upper-crust couple employed as a maid a conscientious, hard-working woman, but the woman's husband was extremely lazy and lived off her earnings.

The lady of the house was more curious than discreet, and finally was unable to restrain herself from asking, "Sarah, why do you put up with him?"

"Well," answered the woman, "it's like this, Missus. I makes the livin', and he makes the livin' worthwhile."

# MATCHMAKERS

A MATCHMAKER TOOK a well-to-do man to meet a prospective bride and her family. While they were waiting in the living room, the matchmaker pointed to the elegance of the surroundings.

"These people are well off. Look at this fine furniture. Take a look at the delicate dishware. Notice the paintings on the wall and the sculpture on the mantel."

The businessman was suspicious. "To make a good impression on me, perhaps they have borrowed these things."

At that, the matchmaker scoffed, "Borrowed? Don't be foolish! Who would lend anything to such paupers?"


A clothing manufacturer repaired to the office of a marriage broker. He wanted to get married. The marriage broker asked his client exactly what he had in mind. The next day, the broker went out and found a lovely young thing that fit the bill perfectly.

The businessman looked at the photograph

shown him, and said the girl seemed all right. But he wanted proof. "Before I buy goods from a mill I look at swatches; and before I get married, I must have a sample."

The broker was outraged. He insisted it couldn't be done, that a respectable young lady would have no part of such an approach. But the businessman was adamant. "That's the way it will be done, or it won't be done at all."

So the marriage broker went back to the girl and apologetically explained the situation. What did she want to do?

"I'm as smart in business as he is," answered the girl. "References, I'll give him. Samples, no!"


A MATCHMAKER PROPOSED a beautiful young girl to a businessman client as a possible bride. The client was reluctant to pursue the matter because he didn't possess, in his opinion, enough money for such an attractive girl.

"Oh, you needn't worry about that," assured the matchmaker. "You'll never have to support any of her family; the girl is an orphan."

The meeting was arranged. Several weeks later, the man complained to the matchmaker. "You lied to me!" he said. "The girl is not an orphan. She not only has a father who's alive and well, but he is living in prison!"

The matchmaker shrugged. "You call that living?" she asked.

A matchmaker was exulting over the virtues of a particular girl. "She is beautiful, tall, well-built, a good cook, a smart woman, with integrity," she listed.

But the client said, "But you left out one important thing, didn't you?"

"Not possible!" said the matchmaker. "What could I have left out?"

"That she limps!" said the young man.

"Oh!" came the answer, "But only when she walks!"

IN A LITTLE TOWN in Russia, there were many more girls than boys. Consequently, the local matchmaker was having an easy time making good matches for the young men of the village, although the girls were often ending up with the poor end of the bargain.

A rather unpleasant man in the village, whose face matched his disposition, wanted a bride who possessed beauty, charm, and talent.

"I have just the girl for you," said the matchmaker. "Her father is rich, and she is beautiful, well-educated, charming. There is only one problem."

"And what is that?" asked the young man, suspiciously.

"She has an affliction. Once a year, this beautiful girl goes crazy. Not permanently, you understand. It's just for one day, and she does not cause any trouble. Then afterwards, she's as charming as ever for another year."

The young suitor considered. "That's not so bad," he decided. "If she's as rich and beautiful as you say, let's go to see her."

"Oh, not now," cautioned the matchmaker. "You'll have to wait to ask her to marry you."

"Wait for what?" pursued the greedy man.

"Wait for the day she goes crazy!" came back the answer.


A matchmaker told a young man that he had the perfect girl for him. "She's a redhead!" he exclaimed with pride.

"You mean Becky, the tailor's daughter?" cried the young man.

"That's her!" beamed the matchmaker.

"You're crazy! She's almost blind!"

"That bothers you? That's a blessing; half the time she won't be seeing what you're doing."

"But she also stutters!"

"That's also a blessing. A woman who stutters will be afraid to speak, so you'll live a peaceful life."

"But she's deaf!"

"*I* should have such luck! With a deaf wife you can shout, you can scream as much as you want to."

"But she's twenty years older than I am!"

"Ah," retorted the matchmaker dis-
gustedly. "I bring you a woman with such gifts,
and you pick on one little fault!"

# MILITARY LIFE

A BRITISH navy admiral tells of the time his fleet was only fifteen minutes into practicing war maneuvers when one particularly inept lieutenant collided his ship with the admiral's.

The admiral knew it was the lietuenant's first command and that the young man was nervous; still, this was a serious error. He wired the lieutenant angrily, "What do you propose to do now?"

Meekly came the return signal, "Buy a small farm, sir."

ONE PROUD BEARER of the flag during the Civil War was only fourteen years old, but he took very seriously his task of bearing the colors of the Union forces.

During a maneuver that ended in failure, the youngster became separated from his regiment. He remained unfearful, however, until a message arrived from his regiment's commander ordering, "Bring the colors back to the regiment."

At this, the brave young soldier sent back a

staunch answer. "Bring the regiment back to the colors!" was his reply.

LITTLE VINNIE HAD decided that the only way to get ahead in the Army was to act tough and throw his weight around. Two weeks after his arrival in boot camp, he stood in the middle of his barrack and loudly declared, "Show me a Sergeant, and I'll show you a fool!"

His words were no sooner spoken when a six-foot-five Sergeant appeared behind him. He glared down at little Vinnie and bellowed, "I'm a Sergeant!"

"Well, I'm a fool!" whispered Sammy.

A MUCH-DECORATED Russian hero returned from duty on the Finnish front where he had performed valorous service. He had been up in the mountains for months on end in the dead of winter. This was his first furlough in a full year.

A reporter came to see him. With a twinkle in his eye, the reporter asked, "Tell me, Captain Ivan Petrovich, what was the *second* thing you did after being away from your wife for a full year?"

Ivan answered without hesitation, "The *second* thing? Why, the second thing I did was take off my skis."

In 1948, when Israel declared its independence, Velvil Pasternak flew at once from New York City to offer his services to the fledgling state. He applied at the recruiting office to join the beleaguered Israeli Army.

After the usual forms were completed, he was told to go down to Section 1 and pick up his Army gear. He came to the first window and the clerk asked him what size shoes he needed.

"Size 8-1/2," answered Velvil.

The clerk looked around in the stockroom, came back and said, "I'm sorry, we don't have 8-1/2. We're very short of shoes. We got size 8 and we got size 9, but no 8-1/2's."

Velvil hesitated, but the clerk advised, "Look, what do you need shoes for? You got sneakers on. It's perfectly okay. Better than to have shoes that are too small or too big. Forget about shoes. Wear your own sneakers."

Velvil agreed and went to the next window, where he requested a medium-size army shirt. The clerk looked around and came back. "Look, we got size small army shirt and size extra large. Medium we ain't got." Then he looked at Velvil and said, "Look, that shirt that you've got on. That's pretty good. What do you need an army shirt for? Use what you've got."

Velvil agreed and moved on. He went through this at each commissary window and came out with his original set of clothes.

He was then ushered into the medical office. The doctor examined him and asked a few standard questions. "Do you swim?" he asked.

"What?" exclaimed Velvil. "Ships you ain't got neither?"

Said the GI to the bartender, "Things at our camp are certainly going great. Why we even have a gorgeous blonde in our barracks."

"What!" said the bartender, "You must be kidding. Is she a WAC?"

"No," said the soldier, "She's just one of the boys. As a matter of fact, she helps around the joint. We bring her food from the mess, and she sleeps in the barracks. She even takes showers where we do."

"My God!" said the bartender, "How does she get away with it!"

The GI winked and said, "Who's gonna snitch?"


THE ADMIRAL WAS ABOARD his flagship in a Mediterranean port. The captain of one of the cruisers made a very sloppy job of it when it was up to him to bring his ship into berth.

The captain knew he had made a foul-up, and dreaded the wrath of his commanding officer. Finally, the message came from the flagship. It was but one word, "Good."

Fifteen minutes later, the confused captain was startled by the delivery of another message from the admiral. It ran: "To previous message, please add the word 'God!'"


AT AN ARMY WELCOMING PARTY, the long-winded commanding general of the base was delivering a boring, self-congratulatory oration. A young second lieutenant, tired of standing, muttered to the woman at his side, "What a pompous old windbag that fool is."

The woman turned to him at once and barked, "Lieutenant, do you know who I am?"

"No, I don't, Ma'am."

"I am the *wife* of that 'pompous old windbag,' as you call him."

"Oh my!" the young lieutenant blanched. "Do you know who I am?"

"No, I don't," said the general's wife.

"Thank God!" the lieutenant replied, slipping off into the crowd.

A TOUGH TOP sergeant glared at the pint-sized rookie and shouted, "What's the first thing you do when you clean a rifle?"

The rookie replied in a low-pitched voice, "Look at the serial number."

"The serial number!" roared the sergeant, "Why look at the serial number?"

"To make sure," explained the rookie mildly, "that I'm cleaning my own rifle."

A PLEBE AT Annapolis sent a long letter home to mother describing his activities. Among other things he wrote, "One of the important things I have to learn around here is how to use my sextant."

The mother looked at the letter aghast, "My God!" she exclaimed, "Is *that* what they teach them in the Naval Academy!"

An officer in the British Army was once court-martialed for being found totally undressed and chasing a young lady clad in a nightgown down a hotel corridor.

At the trial, however, he was set free due to a newly interpreted section of the army rules book: "It is not compulsory for an officer to wear a uniform at all times, as long as he is suitably garbed for the sport in which he is engaged."

The United States has been called a melting pot, and this characteristic is never more clearly seen than in wartime. Americans of all national origins rushed to join the army to serve their country during the Second World War.

One forty-year-old Irishman appeared before an enlistment officer. The Irishman was anxious to sign up. Husky, strong, and in excellent health, the man would make a fine recruit, but the rules stated a top limit of thirty-eight years of age for enlisting soldiers. The eager patriot was crushed.

"Listen, are you *sure* of your age?" asked the officer meaningfully. "Suppose you go home and think it over, and then come back tomorrow."

The following day the Irishman reappeared. "Well, how old are you now?" the officer asked.

"I was wrong yesterday," was the reply. "Sure, I'm thirty-eight; it's me old mother who's forty."

# NEWLYWEDS

THE NEWLYWEDS had just moved into their first apartment, and had decided to begin married life with twin beds. During their first week in the apartment, the wife brought home and placed over her bed the motto: "I need thee every hour."

The husband promptly went out shopping and returned with a sign of his own, which read: "God give me strength."

A YOUNG ARMY PRIVATE was granted a two-week leave for his honeymoon. On the eve of the 14th day, he wired his commanding officer: "It's wonderful here. Request 10 days' extension of leave."

The commanding officer wired back: "It's wonderful anywhere. Return to base."

The earl had made it clear to his bride that in his household he was going to be the absolute monarch. On their way from the church to the earl's estate, the newlyweds rode merrily in the earl's ornate carriage.

About a mile from the church, the horse stumbled. "That's one," called out the earl.

As they approached the earl's estate, the horse stumbled again. "That's two," he stated without expression.

They were pulling up in front of the manor house when the horse stumbled once more. "That's three," intoned the earl. He then climbed down from his seat, went to the back of the coach, took out a revolver, and shot the horse dead.

His bride was appalled. She hid her eyes from the cruel sight and cried out: "Oh, how could you do such a thing?"

The earl imperturbably returned to the carriage and tonelessly declared: "That's one."

The couple lived happily forever after.

THE YOUNG HUSBAND and his bride flew to Miami for their honeymoon, and for days neither hide nor hair was seen of them. On the morning of the sixth day they entered the dining room for breakfast. As the waiter approached them for their order, the bride turned to her husband and said coyly, "You know what I'd like, honey, don't you?"

"Yes, I know," he replied wearily. "But we've got to eat some time."

# NEWSPAPERS

As THE FOUNDER of New York's highly successful newspaper, the *Tribune*, Horace Greeley expanded the concepts of news coverage and developed a high-caliber staff. A dedicated journalist, he had one peculiarity: he was convinced that the word "news" was plural. Though his staff disagreed, he was adamant.

Once, while traveling, Greeley sent a telegram to the home office which asked, "ARE THERE ANY NEWS?"

A reporter responded, "NOT A NEW."

ONE CUB REPORTER was anxious to leap to fame and glory. He spent every spare moment scouting for stories that might be newsworthy, and one day he came across an event that seemed suitable.

He wired his editor for permission to submit a major report from out of town. The answering wire came back curtly, "Send six hundred words."

This wouldn't allow the reporter to expand his style as he wanted to do, so he tried sending another telegram. "Can't be told in less than twelve hundred words," was the message.

His veteran editor was unsympathetic. He sent back this reply: "Story of creation of world told in six hundred. Try it."

REPORTERS SOMETIMES FIND it hard to get appointments with well-known people for interviews. One journalist, however, has developed a can't-fail technique.

"When a secretary asks me, 'What did you wish to speak to him about?' I reply angrily, 'I want to know what he's going to do about my wife!' She puts the call through every time!"

ARTHUR BRISBANE was a very hardworking newspaperman whose column was widely acclaimed. But when his employer, William Randolph Hearst, offered to give him a six-months' paid vacation, Brisbane refused.

Hearst was puzzled and asked Brisbane why he did not want the vacation. Brisbane replied, "There are two reasons why I will not accept your generous offer, Mr. Hearst. The first is that if I quit writing my column for half a year, it might affect the circulation of your newspapers."

Then he smiled and winked. "The second reason is that it might *not!*"

While a young reporter with the New York *World*, Irvin Cobb had a boss named Charles E. Chapin, an ill-tempered man and a harsh employer. One Monday, Cobb arrived at work to discover that Chapin was home ill.

"I trust," commented Cobb, "that it is nothing trivial."

NEWSPAPERS HAVE the tightest deadlines in all of publishing, and unnoticed bloopers often slip through into type.

One small-town editor found himself beset with letters from several town eagle-eyes, pointing out to him mistakes in his copy.

He decided to deal with the problem by printing the following notice in the paper:

"If you find an error, please understand it is there for a purpose. We try to publish something for everyone, and some people are always looking for something to criticize."

Perhaps the most important tenet of journalism is to verify all information. Cub reporters learn that rule when they join the staff; veteran editors instill it in their underlings.

After the Civil War, young Mark Twain headed west to begin his literary career as a newspaper journalist. His first editor firmly informed him that the paper would not print any fact if the reporter could not vouch for its veracity.

Covering the society events new reporters are often tested on, Twain came back with this careful report:

"A woman giving the name of Mrs. James Jones, who is reported to be one of the society leaders of the city, is said to have given what purported to be a party yesterday for a number of alleged ladies. The hostess claims to be the wife of a reputed attorney."

The key to a successful bluff, as any good con man will tell you, is to act without hesitation.

Arthur J. Pegler, a Chicago newspaperman, once uncovered headlines for his paper by walking with assurance into an important bank meeting. He laid down his hat, opened his briefcase, and announced briskly, "Well, gentlemen, let us get down to business."

Examiners going over the bank's papers figured he was a lawyer, and lawyers at the meeting supposed he was an examiner, so they went on exposing the escapades of the bank president. Finally, Pegler rose to leave, and one of the gentlemen thought to ask, "And whom do you represent?"

"Hearst's Chicago *American*," said Pegler, and he hurriedly left to get his story into the final edition.

SIR JAMES BARRIE, creator of the delightful character of Peter Pan, enjoyed his public, but he also cherished the seclusion of his home. In fact, he became furious when his privacy was violated.

An uninvited representative of a local newspaper once intruded on Sir James' privacy. With one foot in the door, the reporter said, "Sir James Barrie, I presume?"

"You do!" said Sir Barrie emphatically, and shut the door.

# OLD FRIENDS

A SUCCESSFUL SELF-MADE MAN was at the bank one day when he ran into an old school chum. "Well, if it ain't my old pal Schlomo Walberg! How's by you?"

"Pretty good," said the friend. "By the way, I'm no longer Walberg. I changed my name to Eldridge."

The other man was surprised. "And where did you get the name 'Eldridge,' Schlomo?"

"What do you mean 'where'?" said the friend. "Don't you remember twenty years ago we both lived on Eldridge Street? Well, that's where I got the name. And what's more, I'm no more Schlomo. People now call me C.R."

His friend was even more curious. "And what does C.R. stand for?"

"C.R.—that stands for corner Rivington."

Izzy thought he saw his friend Tannenbaum walking up ahead of him on the street, so he quickened his pace and clapped the man soundly on the back. "Tannenbaum! I haven't seen you in a long time!" he cried.

Startled, the man turned around. He wasn't Tannenbaum at all. And he was pretty irritated at being thumped on the back. "My name is not Tannenbaum!" he fairly shouted. "And what's the idea of giving me such a hard slap?"

Izzy retreated icily. "What business is it of yours what I do to Tannenbaum?"

Two old buddies, Sam and Irv, met by chance one day.

"It's good to see you, Irv," said Sam. "So how are you?"

Irv gave a shrug and replied, "Ehhh. . . !"

Undaunted, Sam continued, "And how's your wife?"

Irv shook his head from side to side, rolled his eyes skyward, and said, "Eh-eh!"

"And how's business?" Sam persisted.

Irv moved his arms up and down with an unsteady motion. "Mm-mmm," said he.

"Well, so long, Irv," said Sam, as he turned to leave. "It's been nice to see you. You know, there's nothing like a good heart-to-heart talk between friends!"

A businessman was sitting quietly in a restaurant eating his lunch when suddenly a stranger hailed him.

"Hey there, Weinstein!" shouted the man. "My goodness, what happened to you? You used to be short, now you're tall. You used to be blond, and now you're dark-haired. You used to have blue eyes, and now they're brown!"

The businessman was polite but firm. "I beg your pardon, sir, but my name's not Weinstein."

"My God!" exclaimed the other. "You changed your name, too!"

# PANHANDLERS

THE BLIND MAN was standing in front of a building jiggling his tin cup when a woman stopped and dropped a quarter into the cup.

"God bless you!" the blind man beamed. "I knew you had a kind heart the minute I laid eyes on you."

A PANHANDLER WALKED up to a gentleman in the street and grabbed him by the lapels. "Gimme a quarter, mister," he said.

"Of all the nerve!" the gentleman declared angrily. "What's the idea of stopping people in the street and asking for money?"

"What do you want me to do," the panhandler replied, "open an office?"

A WEALTHY MAN decided to eat his lunch in the park one day to catch some rays of sun. Suddenly, an old man appeared, dressed in rags.

"Mister," entreated the poor man, "I haven't eaten anything for three days."

The rich man kept on eating.

"It's three days, mister, that I haven't eaten."

Still no response.

The beggar made still another try. "You hear—three days that no food has passed my lips."

The rich man was quite obviously annoyed as he put down his sandwich. "It's amazing. You yourself won't eat, yet you won't let me eat either."

A RAGGED PANHANDLER stopped Calloway on the street and asked for some money for a meal. "I'll tell you what I'll do," Calloway told him, "I'll buy you a drink."

"I don't drink," said the panhandler.

"Well then, I'll buy you a couple of good cigars."

"I don't smoke," the panhandler replied. "I just want a little money for something to eat."

"I've got a good tip on a nag in the sixth race this afternoon," Calloway continued. "I'll put up the money, you can take the winnings. How about it?"

"But, sir, I don't gamble," protested the panhandler. "All I want is a little money for a bite to eat."

"I'll tell you what I'll do," Calloway responded. "I'll take you home with me for dinner. I want my wife to meet you because I want her to see what can happen to a man who doesn't drink, smoke or gamble."

Mrs. Heckstein was preparing dinner when a beggar came to her door. "Lady, I haven't eaten for three days. Have you got something for me?"

"I haven't got much," said Mrs. Heckstein. "Would you like maybe some noodle soup left from the night before?"

"That would be great!"

"Good! Then come back tomorrow."

A PANHANDLER APPROACHED a gentleman and asked for a dime for a cup of coffee.

"Look at you!" the prospect snapped reprovingly. "You sleep on park benches, your clothes are a mess, and you don't even have ten cents for a cup of coffee. Why don't you get a grip on yourself and get a job?"

"Get a job!" the panhandler snarled in disgust. "What for—to support a bum like me?"

A beggar came every week to beseech a wealthy philanthropist for charity. Every week the rich man listened to his tale of woe and doled out a generous gift.

One day, the philanthropist took the beggar aside and said to him, "Listen, you know I will continue giving you a nice amount every week. You don't have to convince me any more. A little less cringing, a little less whining about your condition, and we would both be happier."

The beggar drew himself up and retorted frostily, "My good sir, I don't teach you how to be a millionaire; and please don't you teach me how to be a *schnorrer*" (beggar).

Mrs. Carey was stopped in the street by a panhandler.

"Lady, I haven't eaten in three days," he moaned."

"That's terrible! You should force yourself!"

# PARENTS & CHILDREN

Royal fathers often encounter the same problems with their children as other parents.

George V of England was a man who always favored moderation. So when the future Edward VIII was attending university and sent to his father for funds, the King answered with a letter that expounded on the virtues of sound financial management.

He angrily explained that he wanted his son to learn the value of money and become a success in the world. The king sent the letter off, hoping he had taught the boy a useful lesson.

Two days later, he received this reply: "Father, I have taken your advice. Have just sold your letter to a collector for 25 pounds."

SAMUEL RABINOWITZ summoned his son. It was time, he thought, for the young boy to learn the facts of life. He took the lad into the parlor, closed the doors, and said, "Benny, you're old enough now. I'd like to discuss the facts of life with you."

"Okay, Pop," said Benny, "what do you want to know?"

A LITTLE TOT had walked round and round the block for hours. The kid had a tiny knapsack on his back. Finally, the cop on the beat approached the youngster and asked what the trouble was.

The kid answered, "I'm running away from home."

"Well," said the cop. "Why do you keep walking around the block?"

"Don't be stupid," answered the tot, "You know my mommy won't let me cross the street!"

A father was walking through Central Park pushing his young son along in a baby carriage. The kid was howling uncontrollably. Everybody turned and stared.

The father merely kept repeating very

softly, "Take it easy, Merwin. Take it easy. Control yourself."

A woman approached the distressed father. She said, "I am a teacher in a progressive school and I notice the way you handle your child. I must say that I admire the way you keep your temper. A fine looking lad you have in that carriage, Sir. So his name is Merwin."

"Oh, no," corrected the father. "His name is Oliver. *I* am Merwin!"

SOL TURNED TO MANNY and exclaimed in exasperation, "Ah, Manny, tell me, what can I do with that son of mine? The boy doesn't know how to drink, and he doesn't know how to play cards."

Manny was surprised. "What's the problem, Sol? That doesn't sound bad to me. Why do you complain?"

"Because," replied Sol, "he drinks and he plays cards!"

ONE HOT SUMMER DAY, Mr. and Mrs. Blumberg took their little boy on a rare outing to the beach.

Mr. Blumberg promptly stretched out under a beach umbrella and went to sleep, while Mrs. Blumberg and David carried on their usual round of verbal and physical activity.

"David, David, come here. Don't run into the water. You'll get drowned!

"David, don't play with the sand. You'll get it in your eyes.

"David, David, don't stand in the sun. You'll get sunstroke.

"Oy, vey! Such a nervous child."

A delighted grandmother was asked to babysit for an afternoon with her daughter's two little boys. The happy trio set off for the park and a picnic.

On the way, the woman ran into an old friend. "How are you?" she greeted her warmly.

"I'm very well, thank God," replied her friend. "And these must be your grandchildren. How old are they?"

The grandmother puffed with pride. "Oh! The lawyer," she said, pointing, "is two, and the doctor is going on four!"

Mrs. Mandelbaum was on her way out of the supermarket when she ran into her old friend Mrs. Rosenstein. The ladies hadn't seen each other for years, so they had much to catch up on.

"Tell me," said Mrs. Rosenstein, "how's your boy David?"

"Oh, David!" cried Mrs. Mandelbaum. "What a son. He's a doctor with a big office!"

"Wonderful. And what about Benjamin?"

"Benny! He's a lawyer. He even might run for office next year!"

"Marvelous! And your third son, Mendel?"

"Well, Mendel is still Mendel. Still a tailor." Mrs. Mandelbaum sighed. "I tell you, if it wasn't for Mendel, we'd all be starving!"

Two LADIES HAD TAKEN a vacation together and were having a marvelous time. They shopped in the morning, relaxed by the pool in the afternoon, and now were getting ready for a sumptuous meal in the evening.

"How about a cocktail before dinner?" suggested one lady.

"No, thanks," said the other. "I never drink."

"No? Why not?"

"Well, in front of my children, I don't believe in taking a drink. And when I'm away from my children, who needs it?"

PARENTS OFTEN SPEAK the truth in ways they didn't intend. When actor Charles Coburn first discovered the joys of the theater at a tender age, he saved every penny and used the money to see play after play. His father one day took the boy aside to give him some advice.

"One thing, son, you must never do," he said. "Don't go to burlesque houses."

"Why not?" asked Charles.

"Because you would see things you shouldn't," came the vague reply.

Tantalized by thoughts of what he might see, Charles hurried the very next weekend to a nearby burlesque house.

And his father was absolutely right. Charles indeed saw something he shouldn't have seen—his father!

A SUCCESSFUL BUSINESSMAN nostalgically revisited the scenes of his youth, his old ghetto neighborhood.

He spotted a bearded elder talking to a youngster and hurried forward to get close enough to listen. He strained to hear the oldster's words of wisdom. "Ah!" admonished the old man. "That's what you say to a grandpa? Drop dead?"

LITTLE HERBIE'S PARENTS decided he was of an age where they should start guarding their conversation.

When Aunt Dottie came to visit, she said to Herbie, "Well, young man, what's new around here?"

Herbie's reply was brief. "Who knows?" said the little boy. "They spell everything!"

A FATHER AND HIS SON were walking through the park, and every few steps the little boy would ask another question.

"What is lightning?"

"Why is the sky blue?"

"What makes trains run?" and so on.

To each question his father replied that he didn't know.

"Pop," the boy continued, "do you mind if I ask you all these questions?"

"Not at all, son. Keep right on asking. How else will you ever learn anything?"

LITTLE HAROLD had come to an age where his parents thought he should know about the birds and bees. But neither mother nor father wanted to explain the facts of life to him. So they decided their older son Jeffrey ought to undertake the job.

That night, when both boys were in bed, Jeffrey addressed Harold in a matter-of-fact voice. "Look here, Harold, do you know what it is that mommies and daddies do at night in bed?"

"Yes, of course I know," answered Harold.

"Good," said Jeffrey, turning over to sleep. "It's exactly the same with the birds and the bees."

# POLICE

In many small villages, some public officials still perform several functions. One constable in a small midwestern town also operates as the local veterinarian.

Not too long ago, his wife took an anxious phone call. "Is Mr. Whittaker there?" a hysterical neighbor asked.

"Do you want my husband as a veterinarian or as a constable?" Mrs. Whittaker asked.

"Both!" exclaimed the neighbor. "We can't get our bulldog to open his mouth, and there's a burglar in it!"

A COP WAS CROSSING Brooklyn Bridge. There was a man perched on one of the girders, ready to leap.

The policeman begged, "Please, mister, if you jump, I will have to jump in after you. It's freezing cold, and while we're waiting for the ambulance to come we'll both catch pneumonia and we'll both die. Please, mister, be a good fellow and go home and hang yourself."


"IT'S AN OUTRAGE the way those nudists are carrying on in that apartment," the old woman told the policeman when he answered her call. "I'm ashamed."

The cop looked out the window and could see nothing but a vast courtyard, a road, and an apartment building in the distance. "I can't see a thing," he shrugged.

"Of course you can't," the old woman replied. "But just have a look through these binoculars and you'll see plenty."


"SOME YOUNG MAN is trying to get into my room through my window," screamed a spinster into the telephone.

"Sorry, lady," came back the answer, "you've got the fire department. What you want is the police department."

"Oh, no," she pleaded, "I want the fire department. What he needs is a longer ladder."

THE MAN WHO owned the corner fruit store had a problem. Every day a dog would come by, steal an apple, and eat it. Finally, the man went to the police station and reported the dog to the desk sergeant.

"I can't do anything about it," the desk sergeant shrugged. Then with a wink, · "He's probably a police dog!"

# POLITICS

ALEXANDER THE GREAT created a larger empire for himself by adding his own empire of Persia and Egypt to his father's conquest of Greece. Alexander thereafter wanted all of his subjects to worship him as a god, in order to help organize his tremendous empire of diverse languages and religions.

Most of the Greek cities had no objections to the trappings of Alexander's religion, as long as he did not interfere in the government of the local city-states. The Spartans, however, were holdouts.

When the Emperor's henchmen arrived to set up the altars, the proud Spartan leaders steadfastly replied, "If Alexander wishes to be a god, let him be one."

LESS THAN THREE YEARS after being elected to Parliament as a Conservative, Winston Churchill braved the voices of the status quo and switched his allegiance to the Liberal opposition. Still only twenty-eight at the time, he had a long political career ahead of him.

He also still had an eye for the ladies, and one day he asked a flirtatious young woman to dinner. It turned out, however, that the lady was brash.

"There are two things I don't like about you, Mr. Churchill," said she.

"And what are they?" asked Churchill.

"Your new politics and your mustache," she stated flatly.

"My dear madam, pray do not disturb yourself," Churchill reassured her. "You are not likely to come in contact with either."

A politician was campaigning in the state of New Mexico. To get the Indian votes, he traveled from reservation to reservation. At one spot, he promised new schools and a new college for all the Indians.

When they heard this, the Indians stood up and yelled, "Oompah! Oompah!" Five minutes later he promised hospitals, fully-staffed clinics, and kindergartens. At this, all the women of the tribe stood up, waved their arms, and shouted, "Oompah! Oompah!"

The politician was much taken by the invigorating response. He told the chief of the tribe that he would like to see the local playing field. The chief said he would conduct him to the playing field where the Indians kept their horses.

Said the chief, "All our horses graze in that pasture. On your way, please be careful not to step in the oompah!"

IN HIS EARLY MONTHS in the White House, Abe Lincoln was busy with many weighty affairs of state.

One day, he went through his mail and found a letter asking for his autograph. More than that, the lady writing wished the President to include some "sentiment" with his signature.

Lincoln was annoyed and sent this response:

"Dear Madam: When you ask from a stranger that which is of interest only to yourself, always enclose a stamp. There's your sentiment, and here's my autograph. *A. Lincoln.*"

An Indiana farmer once took his ten-year-old daughter on a trip to the nation's capital so she could see how her government worked.

After visiting the House of Representatives, the farmer took his daughter to the gallery of the Senate. As they entered, the chaplain of the Senate was starting to talk.

"Does the chaplain pray for the Senate, Daddy?" asked the little girl.

"No," chuckled the farmer. "He comes in, looks at the senators, and then prays for the country."

HONESTY MAY BE the best policy, but often it's quite dull. In ancient Athens one day, two leading statesmen were divided over whether or not to form a navy to fight against Persia.

Themistocles, who favored the plan, was a clever man, though not always trustworthy. Army General Aristides, on the other hand, was a perfect example of integrity in public life. In fact, he was so virtuous that he was dubbed Aristides the Just. He opposed the navy.

It was decided to put the decision before the Athenians themselves. Whichever politician they wished to ostracize—to send into honorable exile according to Greek custom—would be determined by a vote of the people. They would not support that statesman's plan.

On the day of the vote, Aristides happened by a group of poorer citizens. One man, who did not recognize the statesman, asked the passerby for aid in writing out the ballot. The man himself did not know how to write.

"What name shall I set down?" asked Aristides.

"Aristides!" said the voter vehemently.

Fair as always, the General put down his own name, but then could not help asking, "Why do you vote for the ostracism of Aristides? Has he done something of which you disapprove?"

"Not at all," the man said. "It's just that I'm so infernally tired of hearing him referred to as the Just."

A Mississippian once asked Lincoln why he was so kind to his political enemies. "Why do you try to make friends of them?" he asked. "You know they will only be traitors. You should try to destroy them."

Lincoln responded with generosity and wisdom. "Am I not destroying my enemies when I make them my friends? And a friend is never a traitor."

In his early years in Parliament, Winston Churchill once decided it would be appropriate to print copies of his speeches and have them given to all the members of the House of Commons.

Entertained by the pompous gesture, the member for Devonshire sent Churchill this note:

"Dear Mr. Churchill. Thanks for the copy of your speeches lately delivered in the House of Commons. To quote the late Lord Beaconsfield: 'I shall lose no time in reading them.' "

Among other qualities of leadership, John F. Kennedy possessed the ability to accept responsibility, and not to pass the buck when the going got tough.

When Kennedy assumed the Presidency in 1961, a secret plan was already afoot to encourage Cubans who'd fled from Castro to return to their country and to overthrow the Communist regime. What followed was the Bay of Pigs incident, in which all invaders were either captured or killed.

American officials all tried to avoid being connected to the debacle, and there was a lot of name-calling around Washington. Though he'd played no part in instigating the plan, President Kennedy took full responsibility for it, noting:

"It has often been said that victory has a thousand fathers, but defeat is an orphan."

PRESIDENT WOODROW WILSON had a special fondness for those favorite heroes of American literature, the characters of Mark Twain.

On one occasion, when Wilson had to travel through Missouri as President, he requested a stop in Hannibal, the place where Twain grew up. The President wandered through the town feeling nostalgia for his own boyhood, when he first had read Twain's stories.

Chancing upon a general store, Wilson entered and addressed the proprietor. "Pardon me. I'm a stranger in these parts. Could you tell me where Tom Sawyer was supposed to live?"

The storeowner was taciturn in the backwoods tradition. "Never heard of him," he muttered.

"Well, how about Huck Finn?" asked the President.

The local man simply said, "Never heard of him neither."

"How about Puddinhead Wilson?"

"I heard of *him* all right," the proprietor suddenly said with vigor. "In fact, I even voted for the durn·fool."


A RUSSIAN JEW had become successful. He was allowed to travel outside the country as a member of the Russian embassy. In England, he met up with some young Jewish Socialists, and found himself subject to many questions.

"Comrade," said one of the Britishers, "I understand you are a Jew; I understand you are a man of integrity. Now it would be of great interest to me to have your opinion of the Soviet attitude toward the Arab-Israeli conflict. Why do the Russians support the Egyptian fascists against the democratic Israelis?"

The Russian said nothing.

But the questioners continued. "I know your country has an official policy, and so does your party. But as a Jew you must have your own view of justice.·Who do you think is right?"

The Russian maintained his silence.

But the young Englishmen persisted. "Surely you have some opinion?" they demanded.

Finally the Russian, up against the wall, replied, "Yes, I do have an opinion, but I do not agree with it."

ONE UNFORTUNATE community council was forced to suffer through a particularly boring speech about the local electricity generator. The electric company representative was trying to excite some attention by rambling on and on about how electricity had lifted man out of the age of darkness. But it wasn't working.

At one point, he said vehemently, "In fact, let me borrow from the poet Tennyson and cry out with him, 'Honor the Light Brigade!' "

Whereupon one sleepy councilman stood up and said, "Oh, what a charge they made."

The audience broke up with laughter.


Winston Churchill came into his own while leading England valiantly through World War II. On one occasion, the Prime Minister was headed for the B.B.C. to make a radio address when he met up with an obstinate cab driver.

"Sorry, mister. Ye'll 'ave to get yourself another cab," the driver insisted. "Mr. Churchill is broadcastin' in thirty minutes and I wouldn't miss it for all the fares in London."

Pleased and flattered, Churchill stopped thinking of arguing, and instead took out a one-pound bill from his wallet to show how touched he was. But his jaw dropped several inches when the driver's face suddenly brightened.

"You're a bit of all right, sir!" the cabbie

said, adopting a new set of values. "'Op in, and to 'ell with Mr. Churchill."

CONGRESSMAN THADDEUS STEVENS was a fiercely idealistic Republican. In the early 1860s, there was a scandal over Secretary of War Simon Cameron's manner of awarding Army contracts. It was widely held by the press that Cameron was less than honest, and one reporter printed Stevens's opinion that the Secretary of War would steal anything but a red-hot stove.

Outraged, Cameron appealed to President Lincoln to redress his fellow party member for this slur. Lincoln approached the Congressman and asked him to say he had been misquoted.

Stubborn and sarcastic, Stevens replied, "I'll be glad to say I have been misquoted. What I actually said was that Cameron would steal anything, *including* a red-hot stove."

Talleyrand's evil genius as a politician and a diplomat in France during and after the Revolution was exceeded only by his ability to protect his own interests. He managed always to be on the side of those who were in power, and thought nothing of betraying those who had lost influence.

When Talleyrand eventually fell ill and was dying, King Louis Philippe of France came to visit him at his deathbed.

"Oh," cried the fever-ridden Talleyrand, "I suffer the tortures of hell."

Recalling the man's misdeeds, the King remarked dryly, "Already?"


JOHN WILKES, a member of Parliament during the last part of the 18th century, earned a reputation for free thinking and profligacy. Expelled from Parliament twice for libelous writings, Wilkes acquired many enemies during his tenure. On one occasion, his barbed wit was directed at a politician who had been insulted once too often.

"Sir," said his adversary, "I predict you will die either on the gallows or of some loathsome disease."

Wilkes shot back: "Which it will be, my dear sir, will depend entirely upon whether I embrace your principles or your mistress."

THE SMALLEST Congressman ever to serve was Georgian Alexander Stevens. The Southerner was under five feet tall and weighed in at less than eighty pounds. But he wasn't short on wit!

One day, an angry opponent approached him, a six-foot three-inch Congressman from Texas whose bulk blocked Stevens's path. "You pipsqueak!" stormed the Texan. "Why, I could *swallow* you and never know I'd et a thing!"

"In that case," replied Stevens smoothly, "you'd have more brains in your belly than you ever had in your head."

MR. AND MRS. GOLDFINK were worried. All their friends' children had expressed their wishes about what they were going to grow up to be—firemen, policemen, whatever. But their little five-year-old had said nothing about a future career.

"I'll tell you what we'll do," said Mr. Goldfink. "We'll put him in a room, all alone, with only a Bible, an apple, and a silver dollar. If he reads the Bible, it means he's going to become a rabbi. If he eats the apple, he wants to be a farmer. And if he plays with the dollar, he's headed for banking."

So the parents put their boy into the room with the three items and waited half an hour. Then they went in to see what he was doing. He was sitting on the Bible, eating the apple, and had put the silver dollar in his pocket!

"What does that mean?" whispered Mrs. Goldfink to her husband.

"It means he's going to be a politician!"

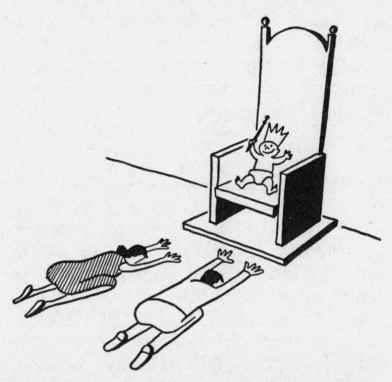

Themistocles, political leader of ancient Athens, was once heard to remark that his newborn child ruled Greece. Puzzled, another Athenian asked what the statesman meant.

"Athens dominates all Greece; I dominate Athens; my wife dominates me; and my infant son dominates her," was the reply.

Our first President, George Washington, drew a hard line between friendship and business. In one instance, when both a friend and an opponent applied to the President for a particular government position, Washington chose the foe. He felt the latter was better qualified for the job.

Some friends took him to task for his callousness. But Washington replied: "My friend I receive with a cordial welcome, but, with all his good qualities, he is not a man of business. His opponent is, with all his hostility to me, a man of business.

"I am not George Washington, but the President of the United States. As George Washington, I would do my friend any kindness in my power, but, as President, I can do nothing."

The power of Benjamin Disraeli's wit was perhaps nowhere evidenced as keenly as in his long-standing antagonism with Parliamentarian William Gladstone.

Once, in a literary debate, Disraeli was asked if there was any difference in usage between the words *misfortune* and *calamity*. He reflected for a moment, then said:

"There is a similarity, but there is also a profound difference. If, let us say, Mr.

Gladstone were to fall into the Thames, that would be a misfortune. But if anyone were to pull him out, that would be a calamity."

CHARLES V OF SPAIN was beset by many problems as Holy Roman Emperor. His kingdom was large and diverse, and very little had been done to organize it.

One day, for some diversion, the Emperor arranged a dozen clocks in a row and spent some hours attempting to have them all tick on the same stroke.

Finally, giving up on the task as impossible, the Emperor remarked wisely, "If I cannot make any two clocks run together in the same rhythm, how can I possibly believe I will be able to make thousands of men think and act alike?"

A MINOR POLITICIAN was once distraught because an unfavorable article about him had appeared in the newspaper. He went to his lawyer for advice. Should he' sue? Or should he demand a retraction by the paper?

The lawyer advised the politician to keep it all in perspective. "My dear sir, do nothing. Half the people who read that paper never saw that article. Half of those who read it did not understand it. Half of those who did understand it did not believe it. Half of those who believed it were of no consequence anyway."

The lady on the plane was doing crossword puzzles, and seemed to be struggling over a few words. In desperation, she turned to the man sitting next to her and said, "Excuse me, but could you help me with this puzzle?"

"Well," said the proper gent, "perhaps I can. What's giving you trouble?"

"It's a four-letter word," the woman continued, "ending in the letters 'i-t.' The definition says that it's found in the bottom of a bird cage, and that the governor of this state is full of it."

The man replied immediately, "The word, Madam, is 'grit.'"

"Ah, yes, so it is!" the lady exclaimed. "Do you have an eraser?"

# PROSTITUTION

Bottomley had gone broke. He had worked hard for 20 years, and finally his business folded.

His wife, Nancy, consoled him saying, "Bill, I'll never let you down. I'll get money for you. You'll start again in another business. I'll get you money. It's no shame to work for a living, and I'm going out on the streets."

Bottomley looked at her aghast. He thought she had gone out of her mind, but after she pleaded with him, and pointed out there was no other way, he agreed.

So Nancy left the house and didn't return for three days. She came home bedraggled, and placed 28 dollar bills and a quarter into Jim's hands. He looked at the money and said, "Who the hell gave you a quarter?"

"Why," his wife answered, "every single one of them."

A WOMAN REPUTED to have been born in Switzerland challenged a number of beach-goers to a race, and proceeded to outswim the four strongest natators on the beach. Everyone was wondering where she could have learned to swim so well.

"Oh!" she explained, "For three years I was a streetwalker in Venice!"

A SALESMAN, told about a very fancy whore-house on upper Fifth Avenue, arrived at the address, and found a private mansion. He rang the bell and was met by a maid who, without saying a word, gave him a card. The card read: "Follow all instructions. Go into the waiting room, and proceed according to the signs."

The client entered a lavishly furnished salon, in which there were two doors. On one door, a sign read: "If you are over six feet, walk in here." The other one read: "If you are under six feet, walk in here."

Being less than six feet tall, the salesman

entered the second door, and came into a small-er, but equally gorgeous, room. Here, too, he found two doors. On one door, there was a sign: "For men under fifty." On the other, there was a sign: "For men over fifty."

Being under fifty, he walked through that door, and came into another room which again contained two doors. On one there was a sign: "If your income is over $20,000 a year, walk through here." On the other door was a sign: "If your income is under $20,000 a year, walk through here."

Since his income was under $20,000 a year, he walked through the second door, and found himself on 86th Street.


During a recent vice crusade in New York, three women of ill repute were hauled into night court. The judge silenced their cries of innocence and got down to the matter at hand.

"What's your business?" the judge demand-ed of the first young lady.

"I'm a dressmaker," she cooed, "and this awful cop . . . "

"Thirty days!" His Honor intoned.

The second girl was in tears when she was brought to the bench. "Oh, Your Honor, I'm a respectable dressmaker with a family to support . . . "

"Thirty days!" the judge barked.

The third was called to the bench and the judge asked, "What's your business?"

"I'm a prostitute," she replied.

The judge looked relieved. "How's business?" he asked.

"Horrible!" she sighed, "With all those dressmakers around!"


A man walked into a brothel and asked to see the madam.

"What can I do for you?" she said.

"Well," he answered, "I'd like a girl who can do it the hard way."

The madam thought for a moment, took mental stock of her protégés, and said, "Mister, we have girls here who will do just about anything. Now, tell me—I'm sure we can satisfy you—but tell me, what's the hard way?"

"Oh!" the client answered loftily. "On credit."


Courageous liberator of five countries, Simón Bolívar was a man of bold daring, and the people of South America loved him.

On one campaign, Bolívar planned to spend the night in a nearby town. A military assistant sent a note ahead to the owner of that town's hotel, requesting for his leader "a room with special accommodations, food, etc., etc., etc."

At nightfall, Bolívar went to the hotel and was treated to a specially prepared meal. Afterward, the hotelkeeper showed the Great Liberator the hotel's finest room, and Bolívar indicated he was pleased.

Then the Venezuelan was ushered into yet another room—in which sat three beautiful girls. Bolívar turned to his host and asked who the girls were.

"The senoritas?" the hotelkeeper said. "They are the three et ceteras."

An American in Paris asked a cabby to give him the address of a good brothel. He went there alone, selected his partner, and ordered dinner. Later that evening, after satisfying his every whim, the thoroughly drained gentleman went downstairs and asked the madam for his bill.

"There is no charge, Monsieur," said the lady of the house.

Astonished, but not disposed to argue the matter, the gentleman departed.

The next night he returned to the brothel and repeated his performance of the previous night. Upon leaving this time, however, he was shocked to learn that his bill was 800 francs.

"Impossible!" the American shrieked. "I

was here last evening and I got everything, and you didn't charge me a sou!"

"Ah," said the madam, "but last night you were on television!"


A man visiting a bordello was warmly greeted by the proprietress. After an exchange of pleasantries, the client said, "And by the way, how is your husband Bruce?"

"Oh," she answered sadly. "He died about six months ago."

"I'm sorry to hear that," said the client. "He was one of the greatest pimps I ever met."

"Thank you," answered the madam. "Isn't that just like life. A man has to die before somebody says anything nice about him."


Harry Robinson had just entered the parlor of a familiar bagnio when, to his utter shock, he spotted his own father coming down the stairs.

Harry reeled back in surprise. "Dad!" he cried out. "What in God's name are you doing in a place like this?"

Old Robinson was equally stunned, but quickly recovered. "Now son," he said, nonchalantly brushing off his suit, "for twenty lousy bucks would you want me to bother your dear, hard-working mother?"

An Army captain picked up a streetwalker and took her out to dinner. Then they went back to her apartment and had a wonderful evening.

Next morning, she fixed him breakfast, and helped him on with his boots. As he nonchalantly walked out the door, she shouted, "Hey dearie! What about money?"

"Madam!" replied the captain with a flourish. "An officer of the U.S. Army never accepts money!"

ITALIAN GUIDE: We are now passing the most fabulous brothel in Rome.
MALE TOURIST: Why?

# PSYCHIATRISTS

In the midst of her psychiatric session, Mrs. Blossom suddenly exclaimed: "I think I've taken a fancy to you, doctor! How about a kiss?"

"Absolutely not!" the doctor replied indignantly. "That would be contrary to the ethics of my profession. Now continue as before."

"Well, as I was saying," the patient continued, "I'm always having arguments with my husband about his father, and just yesterday—I'm sorry, but it just occurred to me again. What harm would there be if you gave me just one little kiss?"

"That's absolutely impossible!" the doctor snapped. In fact, I shouldn't even be lying on this couch with you!"

The lady told the psychiatrist, "My husband thinks I'm crazy just because I like pancakes."

"But there's nothing wrong with that," said the doctor. "I like pancakes myself."

"Do you?" cried the lady in delight. "Then you must come up some time. I have six trunks full."

"I'm afraid I've developed a terrible habit," the patient told his psychiatrist. "Wherever I am, I can't help talking to myself. Is there anything you can do for me?"

"I suppose there is," the psychiatrist replied. "But I should warn you it will be a long, slow, painful treatment, and very expensive as well. But suppose you do talk to yourself. Is that so bad?"

"No, I guess it isn't," the patient agreed. "But I'm *such* a bore."


Poor Mrs. Sanowitz! Her son had been feeling depressed so he'd gone to see a psychiatrist. And the doctor had told Walter that he had an Oedipus complex!

"What shall I do?" worried the saddened mother to her husband. Mr. Sanowitz was unsympathetic.

"Oedipus-Shmoedipus!" he said disdainfully. "So long as he loves his mother!"


"DOCTOR, YOU MUST help me," the pretty young lady told the psychiatrist. "Every time a boy takes me out, I always end up saying 'yes.' And afterwards I feel guilty and depressed."

"I see," the analyst nodded. "And you want me to strengthen your resistance?"

"Certainly not!" exclaimed the distraught girl. "I want you to weaken my conscience!"

A young doctor who was studying to be a psychoanalyst approached his professor and asked for a special appointment.

When they were alone in the professor's office, the young man revealed that he had had a considerable amount of trouble with some of his patients. It seemed that in response to his questions, these patients offered replies which he couldn't quite understand.

"Well," said the older man, "suppose you ask me some of these questions."

"Why, certainly," agreed the young doctor. "The first one is, what is it that wears a skirt and from whose lips come pleasure?"

"Why," said the professor, "that's easy. A Scotchman blowing a bagpipe."

"Right," said the young doctor.

"Now the second question. What is it that has smooth curves and at unexpected moments becomes uncontrollable?"

The older doctor thought for a moment, and then said, "Aha! I don't think that's too difficult to answer. It's a major-league baseball pitcher."

"Right," said the young man.

"Now, Professor, would you mind telling me what you think about two arms slipped around your shoulders?"

"A football tackle," replied the professor.

"Right again," said the young doctor. "But you'd be surprised at the silly answers I keep getting."

A MAN WALKED into a psychiatrist's office and stuffed tobacco into his right ear. "Well, it's obvious that you need me," said the doctor.

"I sure do," the man agreed. "Got a match?"

MRS. HALLAWAY WAS STUNNED to see her psychiatrist running down the street with a couch on his back.

"Doctor Stone!" she cried. "What are you doing?"

"Making house calls!" came back the reply.

FELIX SIMMONS was a nice guy, but a social flop. Although he was 35, he had never conquered his childhood habit of bedwetting. Finally, one of his dear friends told him, "Look, Felix, you might as well know the truth. We're all very fond of you, but nobody can stand to come into your house because it smells, and you're driving your wife up a wall. Why don't you see a psychiatrist about your problem. Enuresis is not too uncommon and it can be cured. Get it over with once and for all."

Felix was convinced. After six months of treatment he ran into the same friend. "Well, Felix, did you take my advice?"

"Yes," answered Felix, "I've been seeing a psychiatrist three times a week for four months now."

"Well, have you had any results?"

"Oh," beamed Felix, "great results!"

"You don't wet your bed anymore?"

"I still do, but now I'm proud of it."


"DOCTOR," COMPLAINED the distraught mother, "I don't know what to do. My son insists on emptying ashtrays."

"Well," said the doctor, "that's not unusual."

"Yes, but in his *mouth?*"


"DOCTOR," A MAN CONFESSED to his psychiatrist, "I'm afraid that I'm in love with a horse."

"Is it male or female?" the doctor asked.

"Female, of course," the man snapped back. "What do you think I am, a queer?"

TWO EMINENT PSYCHIATRISTS, one 40 years old, the other over 70, occupied offices in the same building. At the end of a long day, they rode down in the elevator together. The younger man appeared completely done in, and he noted that his senior was still quite fresh.

"I don't understand," said the younger, "how you can listen to patients from morning to night and still look so spry."

The old psychiatrist shrugged his shoulders and replied, "Who listens?"

PSYCHIATRISTS HAVE BEEN the source of much humor over the years. Distinguished psychiatrist Alfred Adler once gave a speech on the phenomenon of people with certain weaknesses.

Each person tried to overcome his flaw by concentrating all his efforts on it and making that weakness his strength. Thus he described people with poor hearing who became musicians, and underdeveloped men who became professional sportsmen.

When he concluded and opened the floor for questions, a jokester stood up. "Dr. Adler, wouldn't your theory mean that weak-minded people tend to become psychiatrists?"

A WIDE-EYED CHARACTER who was convinced he was Napoleon burst into a psychiatrist's office, thrust his hand inside his coat, and declared, "It isn't myself I've come to see you about, Doctor. It's my wife Josephine. She thinks she's Mrs. Richardson."

ROBERTS BECAME CONVINCED he was a cannibal, and his wife finally persuaded him to visit a psychiatrist. When Roberts returned home after his first visit, his wife asked, "So tell me, what is a fancy psychiatrist like?"

"Delicious," beamed Roberts.

MOLLY AND YETTA were in the middle of their once-a-month telephone call for keeping up-to-date on each other's gossip.

"Oh, and Molly," said Yetta, "did I tell you about my son David?"

"No, what about David?" asked Molly.

"He is going to a psychiatrist!" said the mother proudly. "Twice a week he goes to a psychiatrist!"

Molly knew she was supposed to be impressed, but she didn't really understand why. "Is that good?" she asked.

"Of course it's good!" exclaimed Yetta. "Fifty dollars an hour he pays, fifty dollars! And all he talks about is me!"

MINNIE HAD BEEN DEPRESSED, so she decided to try going to a psychiatrist. Perhaps he would do her some good. She made an appointment with Dr. Oglethorpe, recommended by her family doctor.

After one session with Minnie, Dr.

Oglethorpe realized the usual methods wouldn't work. So he said to her, "With your permission, I'd like to try something somewhat different. I'm going to leave the room for half an hour, and I want you to lie here on this couch and think about sex. Nothing else, just sex. When I come back, we'll talk about it."

The doctor left the room for half an hour, and when he returned, he sat down next to her with pencil and pad. "So, Minnie, tell me what you've been thinking about."

"All I could think of," said Minnie, "is that, at least for me, Saks—even though it's on Fifth Avenue—can't compare with Macy's."

"THERE'S NOTHING WRONG with you," said the psychiatrist to his patient. "Why you're just as sane as I am!"

"But, doctor!" cried the patient, as he brushed wildly at himself, "it's these butterflies. They're all over me!"

"For heaven's sake!" cried the doctor, "don't brush them off on me!"

PSYCHOLOGIST: Do you cheat on your wife?
PATIENT: Who else?

A MAN CONSULTED a psychiatrist for help with various problems. The analyst said, "Stretch out here on the couch. Just relax and tell me about your early life. Just keep on talking. Say anything that comes to mind."

The man proceeded to spill out his life's story. Suddenly the analyst took out a big balloon and, sitting behind the patient, blew it up to full size. Then he stuck a pin in it. The balloon burst with a loud crash. The patient was startled. The doctor said sharply, "Now tell me, quick, what did you think about when you heard the loud explosion?"

"I thought of sex."

"Sex? At such a moment? You thought about sex?"

"Well," said the patient, "what's so surprising about that? It's all I ever think about."

"MY POOR HUSBAND," the woman sighed to her psychoanalyst, clutching her husband's hand. "He's convinced he's a parking meter."

The analyst regarded the silent, woebegone fellow and asked, "Why doesn't he say something for himself? Can't he talk?"

"How can he," the wife shrugged, "with all those coins in his mouth?"

# PUBLIC SPEAKING

Congressman Fred Landis of Indiana was known as an eloquent speaker. He was once asked to dedicate a monument to the beloved American President Abraham Lincoln.

Finishing a beautifully phrased discourse, Landis ended by saying, "Abraham Lincoln— that mystic mingling of star and clod." He was cheered by a rapturous audience.

A colleague who'd attended the ceremony took Landis aside after the dedication and mentioned that last phrase. "Fred, what in the name of heaven does that mean?"

"I don't know, really," admitted Landis. "But it gets 'em every time."


One of the most unenviable positions in life is being last on a roster of after-dinner speakers. One elegant group of guests had already been subjected to a number of dull, drawn-out orations, when the host rose to introduce the last speaker.

"Wilton Lackaye, the famous actor, will now give us his address," he said.

Mr. Lackaye stood up briefly. "Toastmaster and Gentlemen, my address is the Lambs Club, New York." And as he took his seat again, the audience applauded wildly.

DURING THE 19th century, William Gladstone's brilliant oratory resounded many times in the halls of Parliament. His strong Liberal principles aroused him to speak out frequently against the Conservative policies of Prime Minister Benjamin Disraeli. One such impassioned speech waxed quite long.

When Gladstone's address was over, Disraeli dismissed the long-winded attack by remarking to the House: "The man needs no reply. He is inebriated by the exuberance of his own verbosity."

MINISTER AND POLITICAL REFORMER Henry Ward Beecher became famous nationwide for his liberal actions during and after the Civil War.

But during one sermon, an antagonist was bent on heckling Beecher by crowing like a rooster.

The minister calmly observed, "What? Morning already? I would never have believed it, but the instincts of the lower animals are infallible."

DR. V. C. HEISER was being honored by a tribal king in Samoa with a ceremonial feast. All the best native dishes were served, with traditional music and exotic dancing girls.

Soon it was time for a royal speech honoring the Western guest. But, surprisingly, the king remained in his seat and a professional speaker gave the doctor his tribute.

After the speech, Dr. Heiser rose to give his own acknowledgments to his host. But the king placed a hand on his arm and brought the doctor back down by his side.

"Don't get up," the king said. "I have provided an orator for you. In Polynesia, we don't believe public speaking should be engaged in by amateurs."

ACTOR WILL ROGERS followed a pompous and long-winded speaker to the rostrum. The audience was almost asleep from boredom. But Rogers livened them up with a laugh when he announced, "You have just listened to that famous Chinese statesman, On Too Long."

DEMOSTHENES was the greatest orator of ancient Greece, but his political views sometimes riled the assembled listeners who came to hear his speeches.

At one gathering, the audience would not even hear his speech; they booed and shouted so that he could not be heard. Finally, Demosthenes set aside his speech and said he would like to relate a story. The crowd quieted.

"A certain youth hired an ass in the summertime, to go from his home to Megara. At noon, when the sun was very hot, both he who had hired the ass and the owner of the animal were desirous of sitting in the shade of the ass, and fell to thrusting one another away. The owner insisted that he had hired out only the ass and not the shadow. The other insisted that as he had hired the ass, all that belonged to the ass was his."

With this, Demosthenes took his notes and descended from the podium, but the assemblage called him back. The people insisted he satisfy their curiosity with the end of the story.

Demosthenes exclaimed vehemently, "How is it that you insist upon hearing the story of the shadow of the ass, and will not give an ear to matters of great moment?"

The Athenians were abashed, and quietly allowed the orator to give the address he had intended.

WILLIAM MAXWELL EVARTS, Secretary of State under President Hayes, was also an erudite lawyer, and much sought-after as a speaker.

One Thanksgiving, he was asked to appear at an important function. His opening words were:

"You have been giving your attention to a turkey stuffed with sage; you are now about to consider a sage stuffed with turkey."

GENERAL SMYTHE was a member of Congress from Virginia who waxed long and boring when he spoke before that body.

In the same Congress rose a new light, Henry Clay, a young and vigorous speaker, who was liked by many.

One day, Smythe approached Clay, aware of the younger man's popularity. He tried to outshine that popularity by explaining the lasting value of his own speeches. "You, sir, speak for the present generation," he said, "but I speak for posterity."

Clay was unsympathetic. "Yes," he observed, "and you seem resolved to speak until the arrival of your audience."

THE ACID-TONGUED CRITIC Oscar Wilde infuriated those who became victims of his eloquence, although not many had the wit to reply in kind. One day, however, a person in his audience had a sharp retort for him.

Wilde had become so displeased with the way his lecture had been received that he complained, "You are Philistines who have invaded the sacred sanctum of Art."

A man in the front row cried out clearly, "And you're driving us forth with the jawbone of an ass!"

An Englishman visiting America attended a banquet and heard the Master of Ceremonies give the following toast:

*"Here's to the happiest moment of my life.*
*Spent in the arms of another man's wife—my*
*mother."*

"By jove, that's ripping," the Englishman thought to himself. "I must remember to use it back home."

Some weeks later when he returned to England, he attended a church luncheon and was asked to give a toast. In thunderous tones he addressed the crowded room:

*"Here's to the happiest moment of my life.*
*Spent in the arms of another man's wife—"*

After a long pause the crowd began to grow restless, glaring at the speaker indignantly. The speaker's friend sitting next to him whispered, "You had better explain yourself quickly."

"By jove," the speaker blurted out, "you will have to excuse me. I forgot the name of the bloomin' woman."

DR. GEORGE HARRIS, president of Amherst College, had prepared a long speech to give to returning upperclassmen the day before school began. The welcoming lecture was the only event scheduled that day for the students, and they grew restless in their seats and gazed longingly at the warm autumn sunshine pouring through the windows.

Dr. Harris himself thought of the golf links as he reluctantly launched into his prepared recitation, but after several minutes he gave up.

"I intended to give you some advice," he said, "but now I remember how much is left over from last year unused." He left the auditorium to thunderous applause.

THE SCENE WAS A church dinner. A neighboring vicar had been called upon to deliver an address. Unfortunately, the man made too much of this invitation and spoke on and on and on. Everybody was bored to death.

Several notes had been passed to the speaker, advising him that his time was up, but he paid no heed.

Finally, the church treasurer picked up a napkin, scribbled a note, and confidently smiled as it was given to the speaker.

Immediately, the speaker stopped talking and sat down.

The chairman eagerly turned to the treasurer. "What in hell did you write?"

"Just four words," confided the treasurer. " 'Your fly is open!' "


STILLWATER PRISON in Minnesota was once expecting then Governor Christianson to come and address the prisoners. The men were all gathered for the occasion.

The absent-minded governor brightly began his speech. "Fellow citizens . . ." he commenced and then abruptly stopped as he realized his gaffe. The convicts were amused.

"Well," the governor cleared his throat and began once more. "Fellow convicts . . ." he tried. With these words, the merriment in the audience grew more audible.

Exasperated, the governor finally thumped his notes on the podium and said, "Oh, you know what I mean. I'm glad to see so many of you here." Then he turned and left the room to tumultuous laughter and applause.

ONE CONGRESSIONAL REPRESENTATIVE had just finished a singularly witty speech. The other congressmen were fairly holding their sides, they had enjoyed the speaker's humor so much.

After the legislative session was over for the day, however, the more experienced Congressman Thomas Corwin took the young man aside for a bit of advice.

"Never make people laugh," said he. "If you would succeed in life, you must be solemn, solemn as an ass. All the great monuments are built over solemn asses."

Wellington Koo was in the United States to represent China at the Washington Conference in 1921. In those pre-United Nations days, even urbane Washingtonians were not used to foreigners on their soil, and Koo found that people did not know quite how to approach him.

One socialite he sat next to at a dinner party turned to him after some time and brightly asked, "Likee soupee?"

Koo was tired of explanations and apologies, so he just smiled and nodded and continued with his dinner. When the meal ended, Koo was invited to say a few words to the guests. He agreed and spoke for twenty minutes in flawless English.

In his seat again, he noticed his condescending neighbor had blushed deep red and was now silent. With equanimity, Koo turned to her and asked, "Likee speechee?"

# RELIGION & CLERGYMEN

Three missionaries working in different parts of the world came together one year to compare notes.

"I've converted seventy-five percent of my tribe's members," bragged the first one, "and in addition to those saved souls, we've also built a church and a schoolhouse."

The second missionary was not to be outdone. "In my area, I've converted ninety percent of the natives," he said, "and in addition we've built a church, a schoolhouse, and a hospital."

Then they turned to the third missionary. "Aren't you in an area of cannibals?" he was asked. "Have you persuaded them to give it up?"

"Well, it's a long process," said the third missionary slowly. Then he brightened. "But I have gotten them to use knives and forks!"

A non-Jew was walking down the street on a sunny day in September when he saw a crowd of people standing outside a building. It was the Jewish New Year, and the building was a synagogue.

When he came nearer, the man saw that everyone was dressed in his or her finest clothing. Intrigued, he wandered into the building.

There, he was met by the rabbi, who looked splendid dressed in white and gold. "What kind of a show do you have here?" asked the passerby. "Is it good?"

"It should be," answered the rabbi. "It has been running for nearly six thousand years."

In the old country, there was a rabbi who traveled from village to village. In each town he would hold services, and then stay for several hours while the congregation offered him their simple fare and asked questions.

The rabbi's means of transportation was a

horse cart, driven by a sturdy, kindly fellow who admired the rabbi greatly. On every visit, after services, while the rabbi was being surrounded by the congregants, the driver would sit by patiently in the synagogue and listen.

After many years, the driver felt bold enough to ask the rabbi to grant one request. Just once, he'd like to feel the thrill of adulation. Wouldn't the rabbi trade places with him just once.

The rabbi wanted to please his loyal driver and granted the request.

The next day, the pair visited a new town. The rabbi and the driver exchanged garments. The rabbi quietly sat in the corner of the synagogue while the crowd gathered around the driver to feed him handsomely, and ask him questions. The driver handled the services and the questions very well for he had listened to his beloved rabbi for many years and he was entirely familiar with the stock questions.

Suddenly, a student arose and posed a complicated philosophical problem. The townsfolk turned to the driver, expecting a profound reply. But the driver knew he was stumped.

He hesitated for just a moment, and then he scoffed, "Young man, I am amazed that you should ask such a simple question. Why, even my driver, who is not well-versed in the Talmud, can answer that. And just to show you, we'll ask him!"

ORATING ON HELL-FIRE, the minister vividly described the sufferings of the damned. The congregation sat in rapt attention as he eloquently described Dante's inferno. At the climax of his sermon, he quoted from the gospel:

"On that day, there will be a weeping and a wailing and a gnashing of teeth."

In the silence a toothless old lady stood up from one of the pews at the back and shouted, "But some of us have no teeth."

"On that day," the minister roared, "teeth will be provided."


MR. FELDSTEIN HAD gone to shul faithfully twice a day ever since his bar mitzvah. Every morning he lay *tfillin*. He had consulted God every time he took a new apartment, every time he had to decide on a name for a child, every time he had a problem with his business.

Yet when he turned 65, he was still a poor man. What was worse, his brother-in-law had never even come near a synagogue, and yet he was a millionaire! Mr. Feldstein couldn't understand it. So once more he went to God.

"Oh, God, have I not come to you with every event in my life? Am I not your obedient servant? Yet you make Morris a millionaire and me you make a poor man? Oh God, why is this?"

A sigh came up from the altar. Slowly the voice of God came in heavy tones. "Because,

Feldstein, you're such a nudnick! All you do is bother me!"

A RABBI AND A PRIEST were talking one day. They were longtime friends and knew each other well.

"Tell me," said the priest, "have you ever tasted ham? Be truthful now."

"Well," the rabbi became uncomfortable, "once, when I was in college. Curiosity became too much for me and I had a ham sandwich." The priest smiled benevolently.

"But now tell me," the rabbi went on, "and be truthful, did you ever, perhaps, make love to a girl—"

Then the priest began to stammer. "Well, once,when I was in college, *before* I was ordained . . ." he sputtered.

The pair were quiet for a moment. Then the rabbi smiled. "It's better than ham, isn't it?"

As a boy, Woodrow Wilson worshipped his minister father and was overjoyed when the stern man would allow him to come along on visits through the parish.

Later, when he was President, Wilson laughingly recalled the time when his father had taken him to see a neighbor. Seeing the horse and buggy that had brought the minister and his son, the concerned neighbor wondered aloud, "Reverend, how is it that you're so thin and gaunt, while your horse is so fat and sleek?"

The Reverend began a modest reply, but before he could say two words, his outspoken son announced to the parishioner's dismay, "Probably because my father feeds the horse, and the congregation feeds my father."

ONE DEVOUT PROTESTANT had parked his car near the railroad station and was running as fast as he could to make a five o'clock train. Suddenly he saw his minister strolling along.

Out of breath from running, the traveler said a good-day to his pastor, and apologized for speeding by as he had to make the five o'clock train.

"Why, so do I," remarked the minister. "But we've plenty of time, plenty of time." He pointed to his watch. "See? We have twenty minutes."

The runner sighed in relief and walked more slowly alongside his minister. But when the pair arrived at the station, they found that their train had already left.

The minister was apologetic. "I had the greatest faith in that watch," he explained.

"I know," said the parishioner, "but what use is faith without works?"

A much-loved rabbi died a peaceful death, and his soul rose swiftly to heaven.

There, the rabbi was warmly greeted by hosts of angels. They wanted to honor him by dressing him in finery and escorting him through the golden streets, for he had been such a fine man. But the rabbi, inexplicably, wouldn't participate. He covered his face with his hands, and fled from the midst of the celebrations.

Astonished, the angels brought the rabbi before God himself. "My child," said the Lord, "it is on record that you have lived entirely in accord with My wishes, and yet you refuse the honors that have, most fittingly, been prepared for you. Why?"

"Oh, Most Holy One," replied the rabbi, prostrating himself, "I am not as deserving as You think. Somewhere along the way I must have sinned, for my son, heedless of my example and of my precepts, turned Christian."

"Alas, I understand entirely and I forgive," said God. "I had the same trouble myself."

IN SEVENTEENTH-CENTURY ENGLAND, the Church was an important part of family life. In the small villages, the minister was personally acquainted with every member of his congregation and with their problems.

Thus it was natural that, one Sunday in

Shropshire, Mrs. Whitfield wanted her pastor to mention Mr. Whitfield in the morning's prayers. Her husband had joined the Navy and was presently serving His Majesty, the King.

The lady sent a handwritten message to the pulpit: "Timothy Whitfield, having gone to sea, his wife desires the prayers of the congregation for his safety."

The aging preacher, however, had trouble reading the scrawled note. Without thinking, he quickly pronounced: "Timothy Whitfield, having gone to see his wife, desires the prayers of the congregation for his safety."

ONE INTERESTING view of purgatory was held by a mild-mannered Cardinal. He told his colleagues, "Since I believe in the Bible, I am sure there's a Hell; but since I believe in God's mercy, I am just as sure that it's empty."

One rebellious soul wished to reject the faith of his fathers so completely that he felt he had to break all the rules of the religion he'd been taught.

Having been brought up in the Jewish faith, the man found ways to go against every teaching of the Torah. Finally, he went to see his rabbi to tell him what he'd done.

Realizing how determined the rebel was, the rabbi could only ask, "Well, what do you want of me?"

"I'll enumerate all the commandments I have transgressed," said the sinner, "and if you find that I have forgotten any, tell me so I can break them, too."

A long recitation of evil deeds followed.

When it was over, the rabbi said sharply, "There is just one more sin you will have to commit to make your record complete."

"Fine!" said the man vehemently. "Tell me what it is and I'll do it!"

"You forgot the injunction against suicide!"


A WOMAN WENT to confession and told the priest she was having an affair.

"This must be at least the tenth time you've told me this story," the priest sighed. "Are you still involved with that man?"

"Oh, no, Father," she replied, "I just like to talk about it."

THE GREAT CATHOLIC, Saint Augustine, was known for his stern temperament.

Once, a persistent questioner asked him to explain what God was doing in all the years of eternity before He created earth and man.

Saint Augustine's brow furrowed. "Creating Hell," he boomed, "for those who ask questions like that."

Fred Tannenbaum was stationed in a small Southern town. There he met a girl and fell madly in love. He called his mother to tell her he wanted to get married. Yes, the girl was Jewish.

"But you must be married by a rabbi!" insisted Mrs. Tannenbaum.

"There aren't any rabbis around here!" said Fred.

"I'll send you one!"

And so Mrs. Tannenbaum set off for her Lower East Side shul. She pleaded with her old rabbi to go South with her to marry her son. And he agreed. For the occasion, the rabbi put on his best beaver hat, his favorite black silk wedding suit, and his long black frock coat that almost touched the ground.

When they got off the plane, Mrs. Tannenbaum showed the cab driver the girl's address, but somehow or other he dropped them at the wrong place and drove off. Mrs. Tannenbaum, with the rabbi in tow, walked up and down the streets searching for Freddie and his bride-to-be. And as they went along, they seemed to attract a growing following. By the time they found the right address, there were a dozen people behind them staring at the rabbi.

The rabbi pulled himself up to his full height and faced the crowd of gaping Southerners. "What's the matter?" he said. "Ain't you never seen before a Yankee?"

# RESTAURANTS

Two men sat down in a restaurant and ordered their main dishes. Then they closed their menus. The waiter said, "Thank you, gentlemen. And would any of you wish a beverage with your meal?"

One man said, "Well, I usually have coffee, but today I think I'll have a glass of milk."

The other man said, "That sounds good. I'll have milk, too. But make sure the glass is clean!"

"Very good," said the waiter, and he left.

Soon he came back with a tray and two glasses of milk, and said, "Here you are, gentlemen. Now which one asked for the clean glass?"


Steinberg had been having his lunch in the same Lower East Side restaurant for 20 years. Every day, he left his office at noon, went to the restaurant, and ordered a bowl of chicken soup. Never a change.

But one day Steinberg called the waiter back after receiving his soup.

"Yes, Mr. Steinberg?" inquired the waiter.

"Waiter, please taste this soup."

"What do you mean, taste the soup? For 20 years you've been eating the same chicken soup here, every day, yes? Has it ever been any different?"

Steinberg ignored the waiter's comments. "Please, taste this soup," he repeated.

"Mr. Steinberg, what's the *matter* with you? *I* know what the chicken soup tastes like!"

"Taste the soup!" Steinberg demanded.

"All right, all right, I'll taste. Where's the spoon?"

"Aha!" cried Steinberg.

MAX SAT IN a restaurant waiting for his meal. He tapped a passing waiter on the arm. "Excuse me, what time is it?"

"Sorry," came the reply, "Where you're sitting is not my table."

SIR C. AUBREY SMITH entered his favorite posh restaurant and was ushered to his customary corner for a tranquil dinner. Unfortunately, his peace was disturbed when a dissatisfied patron at the next table began complaining loudly.

"What do you have to do to get a glass of water in this dump?" shouted the man.

Irritated, but maintaining his equanimity, Sir Aubrey leaned over and suggested, "Why don't you try setting yourself on fire?"

A MAN TOOK HIS FAMILY to a kosher restaurant. They were surprised when their waiter turned out to be Chinese! What's more, the Chinaman took their orders in Yiddish and even addressed them in Yiddish. The family was impressed.

When they had finished their meal, the man asked to see the manager.

"The food was excellent," he said. "I compliment you. But how did you get a Chinese waiter to talk Yiddish so well?"

"Shh!" said the proprietor. "Don't let him hear you. He thinks he's learning English!"

TWO MEN CALLED the waiter over in the International Restaurant. "We want Turkey with Greece."

"Sorry," the waiter replied. "I can't Serbia."

"Well then, call the Bosphorus."

The waiter did just that.

"I don't want to Russia," the manager told them, "but you can't Rumania." So they went away Hungary.

A gentleman in a restaurant called the waiter back to his table as soon as his meal was served.

"Why is this chicken missing a leg?" he demanded of the waiter.

"I guess it was in a fight, sir," the waiter shrugged.

"Well then," the diner replied, "take it back and bring me the winner."

TWO FELLOWS MET at noon one day for lunch. One ordered chicken soup; the other, borscht.

The waiter brought one bowl of chicken noodle soup and one bowl of potato soup.

"I didn't have any more borscht," he said. "I brought you potato soup instead. Try it, it's good."

So the man tasted the soup and loved it. "It's great. The best I ever had!" And he offered some to his companion.

"It *is* good," said the other man. "Waiter, since it's so good, why didn't you bring *me* some potato soup?"

The waiter was offended. "Say, mister," he said, "did you order borscht?"

HARRY CAME EAST to visit cousin Ben in New York. Ben showed Harry the sights, and wound up the day by taking him for his first meal at the Automat.

Harry was delighted. He gazed at the display cubicles endlessly. His cousin, meanwhile, sat down to eat his meal. When he had finished and cousin Harry was still not in sight, Ben went to look for him. He found him at the apple pie slot, putting in nickel after nickel.

"Are you crazy?" exclaimed the cousin. "You already have fifteen pies!"

Harry chuckled gleefully and continued feeding coins into the machine. "So what does it bother you," he said, "if I keep winning?"

"LET ME HAVE a turkey sandwich," Wilbur told the man at the delicatessen counter.

"Sorry, we don't have turkey today," was the reply.

"Then gimme a chicken sandwich," said Wilbur.

"Don't be ridiculous," the counter man chuckled. "If I had chicken, wouldn't I have given you a turkey sandwich?"

In the posh restaurant, a waiter brought out a bowl of soup and placed it before a distinguished patron who was reading a newspaper. With hardly a glance up from his paper, the patron declared, "Not hot enough, bring it back."

The waiter brought another plateful. Again the patron spoke, "Not hot enough."

Another plate was brought—and again the patron sent it back without touching it.

Finally the exasperated waiter said, "Are

you sure it isn't hot enough?"

"Absolutely," cracked the patron. "It isn't hot enough as long as you can keep your thumb in it."

An epicure was dining at one of the ritziest restaurants in town. He ordered the most expensive dishes on the menu, and a bottle of, fine wine. After the meal he asked for some dollar cigars, and puffed leisurely as the waiter cleared his table. He was halfway through a cigar when he asked his waiter to bring the manager to the table.

The manager came over. The satisfied diner said, "Do you remember me coming in here about a year ago? I ate a meal like this and didn't have any money to pay for it—and you kicked me out into the street?"

"Yes," the manager answered nervously, "I remember that."

"Well," the epicure shrugged, "I'll have to trouble you again."


A man was reading the menu in a restaurant and asked the waitress, "What kind of soup do you have today?"

"Oh," she answered, "we have turtle soup and pea soup."

"I'll have turtle soup," he answered.

The waitress yelled into the kitchen, "One turtle soup."

But the diner said, "Just a minute. I changed my mind. Do you mind changing the order? Can you give me pea soup instead?"

"Of course," she said. And she yelled to the cook, "Hold the turtle and make it pea."


A Scot, an Italian, and a Jew were dining together in an expensive restaurant. When the bill arrived, the Scotchman promptly declared that he would take it.

The next day the newspaper carried a headline: "Jewish Ventriloquist Shot in Restaurant."

A CUSTOMER IN the cafe called the waiter to his table and asked, "Is this tea or coffee? It tastes like cough medicine."

"Well, if it tastes like cough medicine, it must be tea," the waiter replied. "Our coffee tastes like turpentine."

A GENTLEMAN SAT DOWN in a diner and carefully perused the menu. "What will you have, sir?" the waitress asked.

"What have you got," the customer replied, "that will give me heartburn immediately instead of at two o'clock in the morning?"

A MAN WALKED INTO a crowded restaurant at lunchtime and loudly snapped his fingers. "Waiter! Waiter! Over here, please!"

An eager waiter rushed over, and the man commanded, "Bring me a knife and a fork, also a napkin and a plate. Oh, yes, and a glass of water. And step on it!"

The waiter rushed to do as he was told. When he returned to the table, much to his surprise, he saw the man take a loaf of bread from one pocket, a pickled herring from the other He arranged them carefully on the plate the waiter brought, and calmly proceeded to have his lunch.

Outraged, the waiter reported the whole scene to the manager.

The manager approached the man, looked down at him sternly, and demanded, "Say, what kind of a place do you think I run here?"

The man looked up at him imperturbedly, then answered. "Well, to tell you the truth, the service here is pretty lousy!"

MR. AND MRS. GOTBAUM celebrated thirty years of marriage by going to a fancy restaurant. Awed by the elegant ambience, they nevertheless enjoyed selecting and tasting the strange-sounding dishes.

At the end of the meal, however, the waiter brought over two finger bowls and left them at the table. Mrs. Gotbaum looked at Mr. Gotbaum, and Mr. Gotbaum looked back at Mrs. Gotbaum. Neither of them knew what to do.

"Ask the waiter," suggested Mrs. Gotbaum.

"Are you kidding?" exclaimed her husband. "Show our ignorance? How embarrassing!"

"Yes," she said, "but it would be more embarrassing not to use them at all."

"True," said the man. So he called over the waiter and said, "Pardon me, but could you tell me the purpose of these dishes—of—of liquid?"

The waiter was polite. "Sir, those are finger bowls. You dip your fingers into the perfumed waters and then dry them on your napkin."

Mr. Gotbaum waited until the waiter left. Then he turned to his wife, and said, "See, Molly? You ask a foolish question, and you get a foolish answer!"

Seated in an elegantly appointed restaurant, Chico Marx was studying the oversized menu when the head waiter approached his table. The waiter folded his hands in front of him, and with proper continental demeanor, inquired, "And what is your pleasure, monsieur?"

"Girls!" Chico replied. "What's yours?"

A HEALTH INSPECTOR walked into a seedy-looking restaurant and asked for the proprietor.

"I notice a sign outside that you're serving rabbit stew today. Is it all rabbit?"

"Well, actually it isn't," the proprietor had to admit. "There's a little horsemeat in it too."

"How much horsemeat?" quizzed the inspector.

"I swear it's a fifty-fifty mixture," the proprietor replied. "One horse and one rabbit."

Shapiro had had a very good year, so he decided to take a cruise to France for the first time in his life. He was determined to savor every part of the trip.

The first night, Shapiro was shown to his place for dinner and found himself sharing a table with a well-dressed Frenchman. When Shapiro arrived, the Frenchman rose, bowed, and declared, *"Bon appétit!"*

Shapiro replied, "Shapiro!"

This same ritual took place at every meal. On the last day of the trip, Shapiro happened to run into the purser, and took advantage of the encounter to tell him what a pleasant table companion Mr. Bon Appetit had been.

"Oh, Mr. Shapiro," said the purser, "*Bon appétit* is not his name; that's just French for 'I wish you a hearty appetite.'"

"Is that so?" said Shapiro. He couldn't wait to rectify the situation. That evening, at dinner before his companion could do a thing, Shapiro stood up, bowed ceremoniously, and declared, "*Bon appétit!*"

Whereupon the Frenchman rose and replied, "Shapiro!"

A man walked into a restaurant in a strange town. The waitress came over and asked him what he wanted.

Feeling lonely he replied, "Two fried eggs, and a kind word."

The waitress said nothing but went inside to give the order. When she came back with his food, the out-of-towner said, "Thanks for the eggs, but where's the kind word?"

The waitress leaned over and whispered, "Don't eat the eggs!"

# SALESMEN

THE STAR SALESMAN was doing great. Rubin and Cohen were shipping dresses at an enormous rate. It's true that Sid Metofsky drew $400 a week, but he was certainly piling up the orders.

Only one thing bothered the partners. On top of his draw, and on top of a heavy expense account for travel, every so often Metofsky sent in an extra item of $50 with a notation, "A man isn't made of wood."

When this expense item appeared for the third time, Cohen looked at Rubin and he said, "What should we do about this?"

"Well, considering the business he's sending in, we just better overlook it and pay up," answered Rubin.

But the following week, three tabs came in for fifty smackers each, and each tab read, "A man isn't made of wood."

Rubin counseled forbearing, but Cohen lost his temper. "Three times in two days!" he bellowed. "Miss Jacobs!" he called to his secretary. "Send a telegram to Metofsky. 'Dear Sid: Wood, no. But a man isn't made of iron either.'"

A MAN CAME INTO a grocery store and asked for five cents worth of salt. The proprietor asked, "What kind of salt do you want?"

"What kind of salt do I want? I want salt, plain and simple. How many kinds of salt are there!"

"Ha ha," chuckled the store owner, "what you don't know about salt! You come with me." And he took him downstairs and showed him a cellar that contained no less than 40 or 50 barrels of salt. The customer was amazed. "All these are different salts?" he asked.

"Yes, they're all different. We have salt for all kinds of prices and uses."

"My goodness, you're a specialist. I suppose, if you have all these barrels of different kinds of salt, you must sell one hell of a lot of salt. You must really know how to sell salt!"

"Oh," said the other, "me—I'm not so good at selling salt, but the guy who sold it all to me, boy! Can *he* sell salt!"

A salesman fresh from a course in ballroom dancing arrived in Miami for a week's vacation. The first night he was in town, however, he received a wire from his home office that an emergency had arisen, and he would have to return on the morning plane.

He decided to make the best of his only night in Florida. Entering his hotel lobby that night, he spotted a gorgeous young woman seated in an armchair. He engaged her in conversation, and then invited her to go dancing.

The salesman danced impeccably, and the young lady was having difficulty keeping up with him. After about an hour, the salesman decided to be as blunt as possible.

"Look, Janie," he gasped as they danced madly, "I don't have much time. I have to be back in New York in the morning. Can't we speed things up between us?"

"What do you expect from me!" she panted. "I'm dancing as fast as I can!"

A SURBURBAN WOMAN wanted to move from one county to the next. She had a lot of free time to look for a new house, so her husband asked her to sign up with a real estate agent in the next county.

She did as her husband had suggested, and she spent several weeks looking at houses with the agent. But she found something wrong with each one. She never even liked one house well enough to have her husband look at it with her.

Finally, the salesman grew impatient. "Madam, why do you need a home?" he exploded. "You were born in a hospital, educated in a school building, courted in an automobile, and married in a church. You live at hamburger stands, and eat out of freezers and cans. You spend your mornings at the golf course, your afternoons at the bridge table, and your evenings at the movies. All you really need is a garage!"

A TRAVELING SALESMAN walked into a hashery. He instructed the waitress, "Look, I want two eggs, and I want them fried very hard. I want two pieces of toast burnt to a crisp, and I want a cup of coffee weak, luke warm, and practically undrinkable."

"What!" exclaimed the waitress, "What kind of an order is that?"

"Never you mind," insisted the salesman, "just bring me what I asked for."

The waitress went back to the kitchen, told the chef there was a looney guy outside and gave him the order. The chef prepared everything just as it was ordered. The waitress brought the miserable breakfast back to the table, and said coolly, "Anything else, Sir?"

"Why, yes," said the salesman, "please sit down next to me and nag me. I'm homesick."

# SERVANTS

When her maid left service to marry, one lady found it wasn't at all easy to find an acceptable replacement.

She asked the first girl she interviewed why she had left her previous employers. The girl answered that her master and mistress had bickered constantly.

"That must have been unpleasant," the woman offered sympathetically.

"It certainly was. They was at it all the time," said the girl indignantly. "When it wasn't me and him, it was me and her!"

A successful young architect lived with his wife in a large Westchester ranch house, served dutifully by a Scandinavian cook, whom everyone praised as the best in town. One day, the cook, in tears, approached the lady of the house and told her: "I'm sorry, Madam, but I must leave on the first of the month."

"But why?" demanded the wife. "I thought you liked it here." The cook then bashfully explained that she had met a handsome soldier a few months before, and would soon be expecting a child. Eager to hold on to the talented cook, the wife immediately called her husband, then told the cook: "We've decided to adopt your baby."

A few months later, a daughter appeared upon the scene. The architect legally adopted her, and all was calm for another year, when the cook announced once again that she was leaving—this time due to an encounter with a young sailor. The architect and his wife discussed the matter, then told the cook: "It's not right to bring up a child alone. We'll adopt your second baby."

After the arrival of a darling little boy, all went smoothly for another two years, when the maid resigned again. The wife gasped, "Don't tell me that this time you met a Marine."

"Oh, no, ma'am," replied the cook. "I'm resigning because I simply cannot cook for such a big family."

BEFORE THE DINNER GUESTS began to arrive, the hostess cautioned her new maid: "Remember to serve from the left of each guest, and to clear the dishes away from the right. Understand?"

"Yes, Ma'am," replied the maid. "Are you superstitious or something?"

# SHOW BUSINESS

BORIS TOMASHEFSKY was probably the best-known actor on the Jewish stage. He really packed them in.

One night, during a performance toward the end of his career, Tomashefsky failed to appear for the third act. An announcer came to the stage and said, "Ladies and gentlemen, I have very sad news for you. Mr. Tomashefsky has just suffered a heart attack and cannot continue."

A voice from the gallery cried out, "Give him an enema."

The announcer then stepped forward, closer to the audience, and said, "My dear sir, perhaps you have not understood. Mr. Tomashefsky has just passed away."

Again the voice rang out, in raucous tones, "Give him an enema."

The announcer then said, "I know it's very shocking news, and I'm very sorry to have to be the one to announce it. But Mr. Tomashefsky is dead. Your suggestion could not possibly help him."

And the voice shot back, louder and more insistent, "Can't hurt."

After years of working hard and saving, a New York couple finally had accumulated enough money to take a trip to Israel.

They toured the entire country and spent time in the big cities as well. One evening in Tel Aviv, they decided to see what the Israeli night life was like.

So they went to a night club. They enjoyed the singer tremendously. But, unfortunately for them, the comedian did his entire act in Hebrew. The wife sat patiently in silence throughout the monologue.

Her husband, however, laughed uproariously at every joke. The woman was, to say the least, surprised.

"So how come you laughed so much?" she asked when the act was over. "I didn't know you knew Hebrew."

"I don't," said the husband. "But I trusted him!"

DOROTHY PARKER's barbed ripostes cut many well-known personalities down to size. Miss Parker and a friend were discussing a Hollywood actress one day over lunch.

"I think she was wonderful," said the friend, about the star's role in a recent motion picture. "She ran the whole gamut of emotions."

"Well," said Miss Parker, "she ran the gamut of emotions from A to B."

GEORGE BERNARD SHAW's writings made sharp points with which not everyone agreed. Shaw was proud of his general acclaim, but he learned early to deal with his critics.

On opening night, one of his new plays was greeted with such favor that the audience called for him to take a bow. Suffused with pride, Shaw took several. But then one rowdy member of the audience called out loudly, "Shaw, your play stinks!"

The audience held its breath in horror. Shaw hesitated briefly, then said, "My friend, I agree with you completely. But what are we two against this great majority?" And the audience before him thundered its approval.


A New York producer was delighted that Bidú Sayao, Brazilian opera star, was willing to sign a contract with his company. He had her flown to New York to work out the details.

Accompanied by her mother, the star smiled as she entered the producer's office. As he outlined the financial arrangements, however, Miss Sayao's mother tapped the girl's arm and spoke into her ear. The smile vanished, and the opera star shook her head.

The old woman didn't speak much English, and the producer didn't understand Portuguese, but he immediately upped the figure he had offered. Yet the mother tapped again, whispered more intensely, and the girl shook her head once more.

The producer offered more money several times in quick succession, but could not get the girl to shop shaking her head "no." Finally, he could go no higher. "That is my best offer," he asserted. "Either you sign at this figure or the contract is off."

"But certainly!" the girl agreed. "Of course I sign."

The mother tapped her daughter once more. Bidú lowered her eyes, then, and asked, "My mother wants to know, please—where is the ladies' room?"

ONCE OSCAR WILDE set out to review a play that others had greeted as a fiasco. When asked how he thought the play had fared, Wilde replied, "The play was a great success, but the audience was a failure."

LADY MANNERS, a British actress, once told playwright-actor Noel Coward, "I saw you in your play *The Vortex,* and I didn't think you were very funny."

Always one step ahead of his opponent, Coward came back with, "I saw you as the Madonna in *The Miracle,* and I thought you were a scream."

ONE SHAKESPEAREAN ACTOR was approached by a critic after a performance. "Tell me," said the critic, "do you think Shakespeare intended us to understand that Hamlet had relations with Ophelia?"

"I don't know what Shakespeare intended," said the actor. "Anyway, I always do."

A Broadway producer had lured a prospective backer to the theatre to view an audition for his new musical. Sitting back in a front-row seat, the prospect watched each new female potential come out on the stage and display her charms, and muttered at each: "Phooey."

After six or seven beauties had crossed the stage, the producer lost patience and turned to his prospect. "What's the matter?" he barked.

"Aren't these girls good enough for you?"

"Oh," the prospect replied, "I wasn't thinking of the girls at all."

"Then why do you keep saying 'phooey'?"

"I was thinking of my wife."

THE BARRYMORES were a theatrical family, with John, Lionel, and Ethel all pursuing successful stage careers. On one occasion, however, a blow was dealt to John's pride when he wasn't recognized by the salesperson in a Hollywood store.

Perhaps the most famous actor in the family, John wanted to charge some purchases. The clerk blandly asked for his name.

"Barrymore," he stated icily.

Adding insult to injury, the clerk asked, "And the first name?"

Furious, Barrymore became perverse. "Ethel," he said.


SAM GOLDSTEIN had never been to a show in the legitimate theater. For his birthday, his children decided to give him a present of a ticket for the Jewish theater.

The night after the show, they came to visit him and asked him eagerly what he thought of the show. "Ach," he answered, "it was simply nonsense. When she was willing, he wasn't willing. And when he was willing, she wasn't willing. And when they both were willing, down came the curtain."

# SPORTS

FOR NINE ROUNDS the fighter had been taking a terrible beating. Through swollen lips he asked, "How am I doing?"

His second said, "As it stands now, you have to knock that guy out to get a draw."

Sports stars are noted for holding down stupendous salaries when they're hot. The magical Babe Ruth earned a yearly income of $80,000.

One year during the Depression, however, Ruth was asked to reconsider this large sum.

"Babe," a Yankee official worried, "these are trying times. That's more money than Hoover got last year for being President of the United States."

"I know," said Ruth blandly. "But I had a better year than Hoover."

At the turn of the century—before the era of yoga and jogging—one reporter asked New York Senator Chauncey Depew how he kept in shape.

Came the dour reply, "I get my exercise acting as a pallbearer to my friends who exercise."

AUTHOR AND HUMORIST Irvin Cobb never overestimated his skill as a sportsman.

One day, a friend invited him to go duck shooting with some other men. Glad of a day's outing, Cobb went along. The others instructed him to observe silently while the ducks flew onto the lake, and not to shoot until the birds rose into the air again. Nevertheless, Cobb was eager not to lose sight of his target, so he fired as soon as a duck landed on the water.

"Irvin, you mustn't shoot now," lectured the friend. "Wait until the ducks are on the rise. Give them a chance."

Cobb looked rueful. "When *I* shoot," he remarked, "the ducks *always* have a chance."

The young man was furious. He was taking his date to the ball game, and she had shown up an hour late. He'd still not spoken to her by the time they reached the ball park.

"How late are we?" she asked when they were seated, to break the ice.

"It's already the sixth inning!" her escort replied angrily.

"And what's the score?"

"Nothing to nothing."

"Oh, good," she cooed. "Then we haven't missed a thing."

It was a close and important baseball game.

Any disinterested spectator would instantly have decided that an umpire's life is not a happy one. But there were no disinterested spectators present. They were all rabid rooters and razzed the umpire unmercifully on every decision that went against the home team.

But the unruffled ump continued to call them as he saw them. In the ninth inning there was a close one against the home team that set the stands in an uproar.

One wrathful woman vaulted the grandstand rail and with blood in her eye charged on the ump. Restrained from physical assault on that unhappy official by two patrolmen, she shook her fist at him and shouted, "If you were my husband, I'd give you poison!"

"Madam," the umpire replied politely, "if I were your husband, I'd take it."

Coach Leahy of Notre Dame's football team remembers Frank Szymanski, a former center who was the highlight of several seasons. A dazzling player, his manner off the field was generally shy and retiring.

One day, however, Szymanski had to appear in court as a witness. His coach accompanied the player to give him confidence.

The judge's first question was: "Are you on the Notre Dame football team this year?"

"Yes, your honor," replied Frank.

"What position?" asked the judge.

"Center, your honor," said Frank.

"How good a center?"

That one caught Frank off guard, and he hesitated a few seconds. Then he asserted positively, "Sir, I'm the best center Notre Dame ever had."

After the court adjourned for the day, the astonished coach had to find out what had prompted Szymanski's bold statement. The center looked at the coach, then down at his shoes. "I hated to do it, coach," said Frank, "but after all, I was under oath."

Jack Kerns was a respected umpire, except for one fault. He never liked a game to end short of nine innings, even if it extended well into the darkness of night—and this was in the days before baseball was played under the lights.

At one night game in Washington, however, the team in the field decided to play a trick on the ump. With two strikes against the man at bat, the pitcher came up to the catcher and conferred quietly. "Listen, you keep the ball in your mitt. I'll wind up and pretend to throw it. You pop it into your glove as though you'd caught it." Then the pitcher walked slowly back to the mound.

Carefully, he wound up as if to pitch, then he threw a non-existent ball. The catcher popped the "ball" as if he'd caught it. Sure enough, they'd pulled it off. The umpire yelled, "Strike three and you're out!"

Immediately, the man at bat shouted, "Strike? Why you blind so-and-so! That ball was two feet outside!"

MANY A BASEBALL MANAGER has dreamed of the team he could put together if he had all of baseball history to choose from.

Joe McCarthy, who used to manage the Yankees, actually had this dream while sleeping one night, and he says it got quite detailed. He had men chosen for first base, second, third—in fact, for every position.

Then, says McCarthy, the Devil called to him and offered to play his own ball team against McCarthy's.

"What?" said McCarthy in his dream. "You

haven't got a chance! I've got all the good players!"

"Yes," agreed the Devil, "but I've got all the umpires!"

A boxing coach at a Southern university tells the story of C. P. Blaylock, a six-foot-five fighter he trained some years ago. Blaylock's arms were so long that they hung at his side like two machine guns ready to powerhouse an opponent. His description spread among Southern boxing teams, and his competitors were justly in awe.

One day, Blaylock was scheduled to fight a heavyweight from Mississippi State. The first round went by without incident. Then, in the next round, the opponent saw Blaylock winding up vigorously for a right-hand punch. Panicked, he tried to duck by moving inside the big man's reach.

As he did so, the Mississippian knocked his head accidentally against Blaylock's right elbow. The lever action created by this maneuver caused Blaylock's whole arm to fly forcefully around his opponent's head, and the champion struck himself in the jaw, knocking himself out with one blow.

# TEACHERS & STUDENTS

It was the first day of school and the teacher was anxious to get to know her class and have them learn about each other as well. So she suggested that as she called out each name, the child would stand at his seat and say any sentence that came into mind.

She started with Tommy Avery. Tommy stood and said, "I like to play baseball."

"Good," said the teacher. "Now John Bennett."

"I like the summertime because then I can go to camp."

"Harold Cohen."

"I pledge a hundred dollars."


A PROFESSOR OF BOTANY was lecturing to a class of female students. "This branch, you will note, is composed of bark, hardwood, and pith."

The girls stared back blankly. "You all know what pith is, don't you?" the professor asked. "You, Miss Doolittle, you know what pith is, don't you?"

"Yeth, thir," came the reply.

A MATH TEACHER asked, "Joey, if your father borrowed $300 and promised to pay back $15 a week, how much would he owe at the end of ten weeks?"

"Three hundred dollars," the boy replied quickly.

"I'm afraid you don't know your lesson very well," the teacher scolded.

"Well," Joey replied, "I'm afraid you don't know my father."

THE TEACHER IN A tenement district sent Mrs. Cohen a candid note which read:

"Your son Abie stinks. Give him a bath."

Mrs. Cohen's reply was just as direct. "My son Abie ain't no rose. Don't smell him. Learn him."

Young Samuel arrived home after his first day at Hebrew school.

"Well," said his mother, "tell me what you learned today."

"Today we learned about Moses," answered Samuel.

"And what do you know about Moses?"

"Well, he was this general, see. And he got all the Jews together in formation and marched them out of Egypt, with General Pharaoh's Egyptians hot on their trail. And then in front of him, there was the Red Sea blocking his path. So Moses ordered bombs dropped, and bang! The waters parted just long enough for the Jews to get across. And when the Egyptians followed, they were all drowned."

The mother was aghast. "Is that how they teach the story of Moses nowadays?"

"No, Mom," answered Sammy. "But if I told you the story the way the teacher told it to us, you'd never believe it."

Judy was doing very poorly in mathematics, and her professor called her into his office for a conference.

"I'd do anything to pass the course, professor," she sighed, "anything at all."

"Anything at all?"

"Yes, anything at all," she smiled.

"Hummmm," the professor mused. "What are you doing Friday night, Judy?"

"Why nothing at all, professor."

"Well then, I think you might do a little studying."

THE TEACHER ASKED little Morris whether the world was round or flat.

Morris thought a moment, then said, "I guess it's neither, because my dad's always saying that it's crooked."

"WILLIE," THE Sunday-school teacher asked a boy in the front row, "do you know where little boys and girls go when they do bad things?"

"Sure," Willie replied. "Back of the churchyard."


The professors at Harvard wanted to honor the president of their University, Charles Eliot, who had had a revolutionizing effect on education there. So they held a dinner for Eliot at an elegant Cambridge club.

One professor after another rose to offer his plaudits to the work of the well-known president. The last speaker offered yet another toast: "Permit me to congratulate you on the miracles you have performed at the University. Since you became president, Harvard has become a storehouse of knowledge." The other professors cheered.

Then Eliot rose and said, "That is true, but I scarcely deserve the credit for that." He chuckled. "It is simply that the freshmen bring so much, and the seniors take away so little."


The writing-workshop teacher had prepared a special lesson to start off the semester. He wanted his students to learn the basics of good writing through the experience of writing themselves.

So he spent half an hour delineating methods of exposition, and then he introduced an assignment.

"There are four requisites to a good short story," he explained. "They are brevity, a reference to religion, some association with society, and an illustration of modesty. Now, keeping those four points in mind, write a short story in thirty minutes or less."

Most of the students sat thinking about what to write, but one whiz kid picked up his pen immediately. Within two minutes, he was done.

The professor was astounded, and too curious to wait the rest of the half hour. He asked the student to read his story aloud.

The young man read, " 'My God!' said the duchess. 'Take your hand off my knee!' "

A MOTHER TORE INTO her son's bedroom and shook her son who was lying in bed. "Mike," she said, "you've got to go to school. Enough of this nonsense, get up and go to school."

Mike growled, "I don't wanna go to school."

She shook him once again and said, "Mike, I'm telling you, you've gotta get up and go to school."

Mike said, "Why?"

"Well," she yelled, "I'll give you three good reasons. In the first place, I pay taxes; in the second place, you're 50 years old; and in the third place, you're the principal."

IN THE MIDST of a geography lesson, the teacher noticed young Joey doodling on his desk. She asked him to stand. "Joey, what do you know about the Rumanian border?"

Startled, Joey blurted out, "Only that he goes out with my aunt, and my father doesn't like it!"

Two professors were riding on a speeding train when they passed a large herd of sheep. "Quite a large herd, I'd say," the professor of biology said to his companion.

"Exactly six hundred twenty-five," replied the second, a professor of mathematics.

"Good heavens!" the first exclaimed. "Surely you can't have counted them all in that brief moment."

"Of course not!" the second shrugged. "I merely counted the legs and divided by four."

A student went to consult his former professor of philosophy about a problem. When he arrived at the professor's home, he found him in front of the house building a concrete sidewalk.

The student began to present his problem, but the professor interrupted him again and again by explaining to him what a thrill it was to build a sidewalk with his own hands.

As they were chatting, two young boys ran out of a driveway and stomped right through the freshly poured cement. The professor picked up a shovel and chased the boys down the street, cursing vehemently.

The student was aghast at the professor's emotional display. When the professor returned, the student remarked, "Why, Professor, I thought you liked children!"

The professor replied, "In the abstract, yes—but in the concrete, no!"

THE TEACHER ENTERED her classroom in the school on Delancey Street and was horrified to find a small puddle on the floor right next to her desk.

"Who did this?" she demanded. No one spoke.

"I want to know who made this puddle," she said again. "Please raise your hand, whoever did it." Again, no child moved.

So she realized that the offender might be too embarrassed to confess and decided to try another tactic. She took a rag from the closet and left it on her desk. Then she said, "I'm going to leave the room for a few minutes. I want the person who made that puddle to clean it up while I'm gone."

She left the room, closing the door behind her, and after waiting five minutes, she again entered the classroom. But to her amazement, there were now *two* puddles near her desk! She was furious! Trying to compose herself and to figure out what to do next, she turned her back to the class and faced the blackboard.

And there, scrawled in big letters, she read: "The Phantom Pisher Strikes Again!"

One bright youngster was being paraded before a guest to demonstrate his precocity. The guest, who was a history teacher, said to the boy:

"Well, now, young man, do you know what contributions the Phoenicians made to history?"

"Blinds," promptly answered the wide-eyed child.

Children may be innocents, but they certainly pick up on everything they hear. One parent was listening to her six-year-old at her math lesson.

"Three plus one, the son of a bitch is four," he said. "Three plus two, the son of a bitch is five. Three plus three, the son of a bitch is six." The mother's jaw dropped in astonishment.

"Johnny, where in the world did you ever learn to talk like that?" she angrily asked.

"Oh, that's the way they teach us at school," said Johnny.

Unable to believe it, Johnny's mother visited the teacher and demanded an explanation. But the teacher was as horrified as the mother. She had no idea where Johnny had learned those words.

Then she realized what had happened. "I get it!" she laughed. "We teach the children to say, 'Three plus one, *the sum of which* is four. Three plus two, *the sum of which* is five!"

A self-made man was arguing with his son's college professor about the value of education. He thought an education was all right for his son, who wanted to become a doctor, but he believed a liberal education was a waste for anybody else. He was glad he had never seen the inside of a college classroom.

"Do I understand, sir," asked the professor, "that you are thankful for your ignorance?"

"Well, yes," boomed the father, "you can put it that way if you wish!"

"Well, then, all I have to say is that you have much to be thankful for."

# THEFT & LOSS

Bernie was coming down the street when he noticed his friend Moishe coming toward him. But Moishe was walking funny. He had his elbow stuck out on his right side with the hand resting on the hip. Bernie stopped him:

"Moishe, what's with you? I know you and respect you for twenty-five years already, and suddenly you start to walk down the street in this fancy stance. What's going on?"

Moishe looked down at his arm and

clutched his forehead in consternation. "Oh, my God! Gussie will kill me! I lost the pumpernickel!"

Nat was upset. "Irving, I lost my wallet and it had three hundred dollars in it!" he lamented.

Irving tried to help Nat think. "Did you look everywhere for it?" he asked. "What about your coat pockets?"

Nat said, "Sure I looked. I tried all my coat pockets, all my vest pockets, my front pants pockets, and my left hip pocket—and it just isn't anywhere."

"Your left hip pocket? Why don't you try your right hip pocket?" asked Irving.

"Well," replied Nat, "that's the last pocket I have."

"So?"

"So, if I look in that pocket and if I don't find the wallet there, I'll drop dead!"

THE YOUNG NEWLYWEDS had just moved into their new apartment when they received a pleasant surprise in the mail—a pair of tickets to the best show in town. The donor had not sent his name, and for the rest of the day the newlyweds wondered who had sent them the coveted tickets.

After enjoying the show, the young couple arrived home, and found that a burglar had broken in and stolen all their wedding presents. A note read: "Hope you enjoyed the show."

A HOUSEWIFE LEFT HOME for the day and locked the house up tightly, leaving a note on the door for the grocer: "All out. Don't leave anything."

On returning home, she found her house burglarized and all her valuables stolen.

On the note to the grocer was added: "Thanks. We haven't left much."

A South American dictator was building a luxurious retreat for himself and his wife just outside his capital city. A rigid guard was established around the project to prevent the theft of valuable materials.

Each day at noon, the same workman appeared at the exit gate with a wheelbarrow loaded with dirt. The suspicious guard searched the dirt carefully each day, and even had it analyzed by a chemist to make sure nothing was being concealed. But the guard could find nothing to substantiate his suspicion, and, day after day, he let the workman pass.

A few years later, the guard met the same workman in the capital. The laborer was evidently enjoying great prosperity, and the guard was curious. "Now that it's all over," pleaded the guard, "just what were you stealing every day on that construction project?"

The workman grinned and answered, "Wheelbarrows."

# TRAINS

As a boy, Lord Halifax was an imp. Even as he was growing to manhood, he retained a penchant for doing things that shook people up. An ordinary excursion on the train could spark his imagination.

One time, young Halifax shared a compartment seat with two staid spinsters, one on either side of him. Though he was feeling jolly, neither lady evidenced any conviviality, so all three rode in silence for several hours.

The train entered the tunnel just before his destination, and on sudden impulse Halifax made several noisy smacking sounds with his lips on the back of his hand. Then, as they emerged into the light of the station, Halifax took his hat, opened the compartment door, and turned to the two upright old women.

"To which of you two charming ladies am I indebted for that most delightful interlude?" he asked.

Then he abruptly left, and the two women stared at each other, conjecturing indignantly.

The twenty-sixth President of the United States, William Howard Taft, was a calm man, and moderate everywhere but at the table.

Once, when he was young, Taft worked late on a law case in a small town called Somerville, some distance from his home in Cincinnati, Ohio. When he inquired about trains, he was told there would be none until the next morning except for a through express at nine o'clock.

Inventively, Taft sent a telegram to the railroad's divisional headquarters. "Will you stop through express at Somerville to take on large party?" he wired. Apparently pleased at the prospect of the revenue, the railroad wired back immediately, "Yes."

At nine o'clock, the train to Cincinnati entered the Somerville station and stopped. When Taft got on board, the conductor looked puzzled. "Where's the large party we were to take on?"

Looking down at his own broad proportions, Taft smiled sheepishly. "I'm it," he said, and took his seat.

THE HUMOR OF MARK TWAIN was pointed and satirical; occasionally, it took a prankish turn.

At the end of an afternoon spent at a country fair, Twain ran into an old friend at the train station. The friend's sad tale was that he'd lost all his money at a nearby racetrack. Would Twain stake him to a ticket back to the city?

Twain said he was sorry, but he was rather down on funds himself. However, why didn't the friend hide under Twain's train seat for the trip? That seemed to be all right in a desperate situation, so the two men parted until it was time for the train. Meanwhile, Twain purchased two tickets to the city.

When the train arrived, the humorist hustled his friend under a seat, then sat down and carefully arranged his legs over him. When the conductor came to ask for tickets, he was surprised when Twain handed him two.

"Where is the other passenger?" the conductor asked.

"The second ticket's for my friend," Twain answered with a straight face, pointing below. "He's a little eccentric; he likes to ride under the seat."

A ROTUND WOMAN in a crowded subway stepped on the foot of a gent who was trying to read his newspaper. "Madam," he snapped coldly, "kindly get off my foot."

"Then put your foot where it belongs," the woman snapped back.

"Don't tempt me, Madam, don't tempt me," he replied.

When the conductor on a rickety old Tennessee line came through the car to collect the tickets, an old fellow in the back couldn't find his in any pocket. The conductor stood waiting until a man across the aisle laughed and said, "Cal, you've got the dang thing in your teeth." The conductor then puched the ticket and continued down the aisle.

"Cal, you're sure getting absent-minded," the man across the aisle chuckled.

"Absent-minded my foot!" Cal whispered with a wink. "I was chewing off last year's date."

A haughty career woman was traveling by train from New York to a business engagement in a small Midwestern town. When she left the mainliner at a small village in Missouri to transfer to a second train, she was dismayed to learn that she'd missed her connection and would have to spend the night in town.

She asked the aged baggage master about the hotels in town.

"Ain't got no hotel in this town," he informed her.

"Then where am I going to sleep tonight?" the woman snapped.

"With the station master, I guess," the old man shrugged.

"How dare you!" came the indignant reply. "I'll have you know I'm a lady!"

"So's the station master, ma'am," chuckled the old man.

IN A RUSH-HOUR subway train, a gentlman bent over and murmured to the young lady standing beside him, "I beg your pardon, but would you like me to find a strap for you?"

"I have a strap," she retorted icily.

"Then please let go of my necktie!"

# TRAVEL & VACATIONS

MR. AND MRS. LEIBENSTEIN had saved a lot of money and were traveling to a place they had always dreamed of—Hawaii.

But while on the plane to that exotic spot, the couple got into an argument over the pronunciation of the name. The wife insisted it was said with a "w"; the husband was sure the "w" was pronounced as a "v." They decided to ask a native as soon as they landed.

The plane pulled into the airport, the stairs were lowered, and the passengers debarked to the sounds of beautiful Hawaiian music being strummed for their welcome. Mr. and Mrs. Leibenstein approached one of the musicians and asked him, "Do you pronounce your island 'Hawaii' or 'Havaii'?"

"Havaii," said the man.

"Well, thank you," said Mr. Leibenstein, and he smiled smugly.

"You're velcome," said the musician.

Though the practice of discrimination in major hotels has declined, many elegant establishments in years past used to bar members of minority groups from registering.

On one occasion, American musical composer George M. Cohan wired ahead for reservations at an exclusive hotel in a city he was planning to visit. Presuming from his name that he was Jewish, the hotel promptly sent back an answering wire. Its clientele was very exclusive, the hotel said, and it therefore could not accommodate him.

Cohan was outraged. Though he was not Jewish, the blatant discrimination infuriated him. He immediately sent back another wire:

"Apparently, there has been a mistake on both sides: You thought I was Jewish and I thought you were gentlemen."

ONE VETERAN OF Miami Beach had been coming every winter for twenty years. One day, she spotted an old friend from New York on the beach.

"Sadie!" she called out. "It's so good to see you! How are you?"

"Molly!" cried the other. "Actually I'm not feeling so good. That's why I came down here for a week."

Molly thought for a minute, then she asked discreetly, "Darling, have you been through the menopause yet?"

Sadie looked at her. "The Menopause? I told you I just arrived. I haven't even been through the Fountainbleau yet!"

AFTER THE UNITED STATES launched its space program, the astronauts became overnight heroes. Everyone spoke of their accomplishments.

Two feisty Jewish ladies were indulging in their morning chat and one remarked, "Bessie, did you hear about the astronauts? I understand they went around the world several times!"

The other lady was not impressed. "Big deal!" she sniffed. "If you have money, you can afford to travel."

The traveller's car stopped suddenly on a lonely road, far from any town. A quick look showed him that he'd run out of gasoline. As night fell, he made his way towards a light in the distance, and came upon a small house off the side of the road. A knock on the door was answered by a beautiful young woman.

"Pardon me, madam," the traveller began, "but my car has run out of gas. Do you think you could put me up for the night here?"

After much coaxing, the young lady finally consented to allow the traveller to stay, and escorted·him to a neat little room on the second floor.

While preparing for bed, the motorist couldn't help thinking of his hostess and the flimsy nightgown she wore. At last, he crawled into bed with a sigh, but couldn't sleep. Before long, the sheets assumed the form of a tent above him. Then there was a sudden rapping at his door.

"Yes?" he called out hopefully. The smiling face of his hostess showed itself in the doorway.

"Would you like company?" the lady whispered softly.

"Company?" the guest shouted. "You bet I would!"

"That's good," the lady replied, "because another gentleman who's run out of gas is at the door and wants me to put him up too!"

A REAL DOWN-HOME AMERICAN, MARK TWAIN held no airs for royalty, and his reaction to its members was often tinged with humor.

Once, Twain checked into a hotel and was asked to sign the register. He saw that the arrival just before him was a titled man who had registered, "Baron von So-and-so and valet."

Twain took pen in hand and scrawled his own entry in the register. "Mark Twain and valise," he wrote.

Sam Silverman had worked for most of his life in a Seventh Avenue sweatshop. During every February, when the days were wan and chilly, the members of Sam's union took a three-week vacation without pay, and went down to Miami.

They would come home with glowing stories. Sam dreamed of the day when he could afford to take such a marvelous trip to avoid the winter's cold.

In five years, Sam had saved up enough money to request an unpaid vacation. His request was granted. He flew down to Miami, registered in a small hotel, and stepped out into the full glare of Collins Avenue for a stroll. Then he sat down on one of the benches, to admire the beautiful palm trees. Within minutes, a woman sat down right beside him. She opened with a few questions, a conversation ensued, and the two soon became real chummy. Within an hour, they were in Sam's room, and they didn't emerge —neither of them—for three days.

Sam had the most wonderful time of his life. He came home ecstatic. Now he didn't mind his work, he was so full of memories of that marvelous vacation in Miami.

About four weeks later, a man called at the sweatshop and asked for Sam Silverman. The man was dressed in a dark gray suit, carried a briefcase, and had a business air about him. When Sam was pointed out, the man went straight to him, and said, "Are you Mr. Silverman?"

Sam said, "Yes, I'm Silverman."

"Well," said the man, looking him straight up and down, "I've got something I'd like to show you." He opened his briefcase, and spread on Sam's table six photographs which revealed Sam in the most compromising positions. Nude, Sam was rolling in bed with his lady-love, in that hotel room in Miami.

Sam looked at the pictures a moment, and then his face broke into a beautiful smile. "Mister," he said, "I'll take two of these, three of that, one of those, and four of this one!"


CUSTOMS OFFICIALS are like doctors—they see people's most personal belongings, and they have to be prepared for anything.

One woman at Kennedy Airport insisted she had bought nothing abroad.

"Are you quite sure that you have nothing to declare?" the customs agent asked her.

"Absolutely sure," she said firmly.

"Am I to understand, then," smiled the agent, "that the fur tail hanging from under your dress is your own?"


An old gent was going to the mountains for the first time in his life. He was poor, so he had to go by bus, but that didn't dent his spirit. He was so happy that he began singing as soon as he boarded the crowded vehicle.

The driver had been going for many hours, and wasn't too pleased about having the old man standing in the aisle right behind him, singing at the top of his lungs. And he told him so.

But the singing didn't stop; and after several vain exhortations, the driver warned the man that if he didn't cut out the singing, he'd stop the bus and toss out his valise. Even this threat didn't quiet the old man. Fifteen minutes later, the driver pulled off the road, walked up to the old man, picked up the valise, and threw it out the nearest window.

Then the driver returned to his seat. But the singing continued. Finally the driver listened to the words: "I'm going to the mountains! I'm going to the mountains! I won't call the police! I didn't bring a valise!"


On the first day of her Miami vacation, a beautifully proportioned young lady went up to the roof of her hotel to acquire a suntan as quickly as possible. Discovering there was not another soul on the roof, she slipped her bathing suit off and stretched out, face downward, with only a small towel stretched across her back.

Suddenly a flustered assistant manager of the hotel dashed onto the roof and gasped apologetically, "Miss, we don't mind if you sun on the roof, but we must ask you to keep your bathing suit on."

"What difference does it make?" the young lady demanded. "No one can see me up here, and I've covered my back with a towel."

"Of course," the assistant manager conceded, "but unfortunately you are lying on the dining room skylight."

ONE MIDWESTERN BUSINESSMAN will not easily forget the time he was to attend a convention in Paris. He went all the way out to the airport, arriving less than an hour before his flight departed, when he suddenly realized he had only American money in his wallet.

Quickly, he dashed to a nearby phone and called his secretary, who was nice to look at, but rather inexperienced in business matters. "Susie!" he exclaimed into the phone. "Get me fifty dollars' worth of francs and hurry out here as fast as you can!"

Twenty minutes later, a cab screeched to a halt at the terminal and Susie leaped out—carrying two hundred hot dogs.

# VANITY

Newspaperman Horace Greeley once spent three months serving in Congress.

In conversation one day during that time, a fellow legislator puffed himself up and announced pompously, "I am a self-made man."

To this remark Greeley replied, "That, sir, relieves the Almighty of a great responsibility."


At a recent dinner party, a woman spoke to the man seated on her right and said that men were much vainer than women. The gentleman thought that idea was preposterous, and that vanity was a trait unheard of in men.

The woman said, "I'll prove it to you. Watch."

Then she raised her voice several degrees and said quite firmly, "It's a shame that most intelligent and sensitive men attach so little importance to the way they dress. Why, right this minute, the most cultivated man in this room is wearing the most clumsily knotted tie."

She easily won her point when every man's hand suddenly flew to his neck.

One awkward adolescent visited her priest and shyly told him she thought she'd committed the sin of vanity.

"What makes you think that?" the Father inquired.

"Every morning when I look into the mirror," she said, embarrassed, "I think how beautiful I am."

"Never fear, my girl," said the strict Father. "That isn't a sin; it's only a mistake."

The choice of words we make is often of utmost importance to our listeners.

Trying to reach a top-shelf book one day, Napoleon was stymied by his inability to stretch his arm far enough. An extremely tall marshal came to his aid and took the book down, saying to his Emperor, "Permit me, sir—I am higher than Your Majesty."

Napoleon angrily grumbled, "Marshal, you are longer."

George Gershwin, pleased with himself, was once rhapsodizing about his latest musical score to some of his friends, among them dry-humored Oscar Levant.

Levant said nothing while Gershwin spoke. Then he asked, "George, if you had it to do over, would you fall in love with yourself again?"

SAM GOLDWYN didn't get to be king of Hollywood by being indecisive. When asked why he wouldn't change his mind about a particular script, Goldwyn asserted, "I'm willing to admit that I may not always be right—but I'm never wrong."

President Charles de Gaulle led his country with patriotism and zeal for many years, but the General was also a rather stiff man who observed every formality. A story is told that one winter night upon retiring, his wife shivered and said, "My God, it's cold."

Yielding slightly, De Gaulle replied, "In bed, Madame, you may call me Charles."

# WAGERS

The twenty-ninth President of the United States, Calvin Coolidge, was a reticent man, never known for scintillating conversation.

A socialite once sat next to him at a party and babbled, "Oh, Mr. President, do you know I made a bet today that I would get more than two words out of you?"

Maintaining his reserve, Collidge responded quietly, "You lose."

Izzy's friend Yosef said he had found a parrot that not only would speak, but could speak Hebrew. Izzy was skeptical, but when he went to Yosef's house, they put a yarmulke on the bird's head, and the parrot immediately recited the full Friday night services.

Izzy was amazed, and begged his friend to let him buy the bird. After much cajoling, Yosef agreed. For the price of ten dollars, Izzy was able to take away the *dovvining* bird.

On Rosh Hashonah, Izzy took his bird to the synagogue. He passed the word around that his parrot could sing the prayers. Everyone laughed at his pretensions, and he extracted wagers of 10 to 1 that his bird couldn't follow the service for even three minutes.

When the prayers began, Izzy put a yarmulke on the parrot's head and commanded him to sing. But the bird was silent.

"Go, pray, like you did for Yosef," Izzy urged. But the parrot wouldn't open its beak.

"Pray, you numbskull! I have a bet on you!" But the parrot wouldn't utter a sound. Finally, Izzy had to admit defeat, and left the synagogue downcast and deep in debt.

When he got home, he lashed into the bird. "So you shame me in front of everybody, eh? So you make me lose ten to one bets? So you pretend you don't know how to pray? Why did you do that?"

Finally, the parrot spoke up. "Don't be stupid!" said the parrot. "Comes Yom Kippur, you'll make a killing!"